The Landowners

MULLER

THE LANDOWNERS

Douglas Sutherland

MULLER
London Melbourne Auckland Johannesburg

First published in Great Britain in 1968 by Anthony Blond Ltd.
This revised edition published in 1988 by
Frederick Muller, an imprint of
Century Hutchinson Ltd, Brookmount House, 62–65 Chandos Place,
London WC2N 4NW

Century Hutchinson Australia Pty Ltd
PO Box 496, 16–22 Church Street, Hawthorn, Victoria 3122, Australia

Century Hutchinson New Zealand Limited
PO Box 40–086, Glenfield, Auckland 10, New Zealand

Century Hutchinson South Africa Pty Ltd
PO Box 337, Bergvlei, 2021 South Africa

British Library Cataloguing in Publication Data

Sutherland, Douglas, 1919–
   The landowners.—2nd ed
   1. Great Britain. Land. Ownership
   I. Title
   333.3′0941
   ISBN 0 09 713678 1

Photoset by Deltatype Ltd, Ellesmere Port
Printed in Great Britain by Butler & Tanner Ltd, Frome and London

Contents

For Harriet Wye

List of Illustrations

Five generations of a traditional landowning family: the Milbanks of Barningham Park, Yorkshire

Sir David Montgomery
Lord Mansfild

Castle Howard, Yorkshire

The Duke of Westminster

The Maktoum brothers at Ascot
The Ritz Hotel

Chatsworth, Derbyshire

Sandringham, Norfolk
The Duke of Roxburghe

Eaton Hall
Drum Castle

Introduction

An elderly professor at an ancient university was asked whether he had noticed much change over the years in the examination of graduation students.

His reply was, 'The questions asked today are still the same. It is only the answers which have changed.'

When I first brought out this book, over twenty years ago, my aim was to present as comprehensive a survey of who owned what, and how they had acquired it, as was possible in a single volume covering such a vast field. The ownership of land in Britain has always been, as it has been in most countries in the world, the cornerstone of power and the foundation of the economy. When Professor G. M. Trevelyan described the Industrial Revolution of the nineteenth century as 'by far the most important movement in social history since the Saxon conquest' he was certainly stating the truth. It changed the nation from being an agricultural one in which the power of the great landowners was complete to a great industrial one – at the time the greatest industrial nation in the world; but the Industrial Revolution was only made possible by the Agricultural Revolution which preceded it and which had completely changed the face of the countryside. The great landowners who owed their survival for over a thousand years to their ability to adapt to changing conditions remained as firmly entrenched behind their high park walls as ever.

Today the question of survival is perhaps more topical than it has ever been but, although the questions remain the same, the answers have changed out of all recognition – more so than ever since the first edition of *The Landowners* was published. This is due in the main to the increasingly diverse demands made upon land and, consequently, the landholder – demands as diverse as forestry, urban development, sporting rights, public access and, perhaps above all, the changing demands for the agricultural product both in Britain and inside the Common Market. It is under these pressures that the shape of landownership is changing both in its traditional role as a perquisite of great landlords, including the Church and the Crown, and as an investment for institutions ranging from City capitalists to the trade unions.

In this updated version I have tried to show the changing role of land in the national economy and to point the direction in which we are heading – without, of course, providing any of the answers. Those

perhaps will be, and indeed to a degree already are being, provided by
the landowners themselves.

Douglas Sutherland
Foscote
1987

1
The Eighteenth Century

England at the beginning of the eighteenth century presented a picture which would seem strange indeed to modern eyes. Almost the whole of the national economy depended on the land. The first rumblings of the Industrial Revolution had still to be heard, and such industry as there was remained dispersed in small villages. Bradford was a village which had still to find its future as the centre of the wool trade, and Manchester was not very much larger. Wigan was a fashionable spa, and Yarmouth one of the most important ports in the country. The P & O shipping line operated from the busy West Cumberland port of Whitehaven, and the slave ships were running from the less well-known port of Liverpool. London was largely confined within the old city gates. The grandees built their houses along the banks of the Thames at Westminster, thus combining the advantages of both a town and a country residence, for they could still hunt a fox in Hampstead and shoot wildfowl where Belgrave Square now stands. Less than a quarter of the total population led urban lives and more people were employed in working with horses than in any other business.

Communications were difficult and often dangerous. Such roads as there were were rutted and potholed so that in wet weather they were almost impassable. Canals and railways to meet the needs of industry were still in the future so that it was only the very rich and important who could afford the luxury of family travel. To transport goods inland was immensely expensive. To burn coal cost four times as much in the country as it did in a seaport.

The countryside itself was very different from the highly cultivated scene which it presents today. Much of it was undrained, and much more was scrub and wasteland. The Agricultural Revolution which was to pave the way for the Industrial Revolution, and change the face of the English countryside, was not to gather impetus until the second half of the century. It was only with the enclosure of land that the familiar English hedgerows came into being, and few people had thought to plant trees either for profit or to beautify the countryside. The great forests of earlier centuries were growing smaller, but where they existed they were dense and impenetrable. Agriculture relied on traditional methods which were both wasteful and uneconomic. The poor who worked the land were very poor indeed and the rich, who owned it, held all the power.

The main source of wealth was the land, so that to own land was to have a share of the equity which not only produced dividends but gave the holder a say in the running of affairs. To be landless was to be merely a hired servant with no security and no rights. This was the heyday of the great landowners. They were not only the board of directors, but they also held all the shares.

To own land in the eighteenth century was the very cornerstone of power. The days when a wrong political view could cost an ambitious baron his lands, and often his head as well, were past. By the time Queen Anne was on the throne, the great upheaval caused by Cromwell's revolution had largely worked itself out. It is true that the country was at war with France and that the wars of the Hanoverian Succession were still to come; there were to be the Scottish rebellions of 1715 and 1745, too, and revolution in France and America. But with the accession to the throne of England of the Dutch William of Orange followed, after the death of his sister-in-law Queen Anne, by the successive German Georges, much of the power of the monarchy passed into the hands of the established English aristocracy whose influence in the conduct of affairs was now so formidable that it seemed unlikely it could ever be broken. The English landowner was never to feel more settled and secure.

To be a big landowner was to be something, but to be a peer of the realm as well was to be everything. By no means all the big landowners were peers, but all the peers were big landowners, and it was in their hands that the greatest power rested. They had, of course, a monopoly of power in the House of Lords, but their influence in the House of Commons was more than formidable. Even as late as the mid-nineteenth centry it is estimated that at least two-thirds of the elected members sat in the landed interest. The peers themselves held many of the high offices of state, and those which they did not occupy were parcelled out to reliable friends or relations.

This concentration of power is all the more impressive when it is realized that the number of the peerage was very small indeed. Until the younger Pitt realized the political advantage to be gained in creating new peerages, there were only between 160 and 170, excluding Irish peerages which did not count as they did not carry with them a seat in the House of Lords anyway. They were an exclusive body of men, and determined to remain so. Their unwillingness to open their ranks to newcomers was demonstrated by their attempt in 1719 to introduce the Peerage Bill, designed to limit the number of peers which could be created and thus to preserve the exclusivity of the peerage by law. Although the bill was rejected by the Commons this did not alter the fact that the aristocracy was an extremely select club in which all the members were land-rich and becoming richer. Everybody in the club knew everybody else, and most were related by marriage.

The power of the aristocratic landowner in his own territory was absolute. To be a peer was to be above the law. A peer could not be arrested for debt, have his estates impounded, or be declared a bankrupt. He was privileged to an amazing degree. He paid fewer taxes than the commoner, and lighter tolls at the turnpike. He sent his letters post-free and, if he felt so inclined, could frank the letters of his friends for nothing. His person was sacrosanct. To quote *The Black Book**: 'You may knock down Nathan Rothschild, though he is a very rich man, or a worshipful alderman, or even a right honourable lord mayor, and the justices will only charge you a few shillings for the liberty you have taken; but if you knock down a peer, though he is ever so insolent, it is almost as bad as murder.'

It was not surprising that the workman in the fields accepted without question that he was less than dust under the feet of so splendid a person. And not only the workman in the fields: the local tradesmen sought the aristocratic landowner's patronage as assiduously as if he were the king himself. Even the wealthy squirearchy vied with one another to insinuate themselves in his good graces, and an invitation to his house was a rare honour.

There was no part of the life of the countryside which was not presided over by the aristocracy. They intruded into religious life because they had control of the livings of the clergy. As William Cowper wrote in 1783: 'The Parson knows enough who knows a Duke.' They controlled secular life because they appointed the justices of the peace to administer the law; and their economic hold over the life of the community was complete. On their predisposition to tyranny or benign feudalism the whole welfare of their inferiors depended.

Undoubtedly there was abuse, but, on balance, the most surprising thing is how limited it was. It would be quite wrong to present a picture of the hierarchy of great landowners as a group of power-drunk men who were careless of their responsibilities. The Comte de Montal-embert, who had watched the eclipse of the French aristocracy, wrote:

> The true strength of the English Aristocracy and nationality abides in the many thousands of families of Landed Proprietors who are the magistrates and administrators of the country. They do not disdain, as the old French nobility did, to accept administrative, legislative and judicial functions. Far

---

* J. Wade, *The Black Book or Corruption Unmasked!!!* First published in 1820, and brought up to date in later editions, this was a savage attack on abuses of the times. As Helen Bosanquet remarks, that Wade 'is not free from prejudice seems obvious, but it is impossible to question the basis of truth in his accusations'.

from it – they have almost monopolised them, and by so doing have maintained themselves as the head of all the developments of society.

Add to this observation Edmund Burke's view of the landed interest as 'a partnership not only between those who are living, but between those who are living, those who are dead, and those who are to be born', and we have a realistic picture of the sense of responsibility which imbued the greater number by far of English landowners. One can have sympathy with the generally accepted view of the owner of an inherited estate, that he held it for his lifetime in trust for his heirs and that it was his duty to pass on a better or at least as good a heritage as that to which he himself had been heir. The rule of primogeniture by which most of the big estates have been kept intact is an expression of this philosophy. The English landowner, however, had a sense of responsibility which extended far beyond the family circle or the boundaries of his estate. Although it is true that even the greatest families amongst the great, like the Howards, the Russells and the Cavendishes, occupied themselves assiduously in the collection of family honours and even further riches to reinforce their seemingly impregnable position, they were – unlike their European and, perhaps especially, their Russian counterparts – conscious of their duty to work actively for the preservation of society as a whole.

How well Oliver Goldsmith describes the contented rustic scene, unique to England, in *The Deserted Village*.

How often have I loitered o'er the green,
Where humble happiness endeared each scene!
How often have I paused on every charm,
The sheltered cot, the cultivated farm,
The never-failing brook, the busy mill,
The decent church that topped the neighbouring hill,
The hawthorn bush, with seats beneath the shade,
For talking age and whispering lovers made.

However, by the time Goldsmith died in 1774 the first shiver of a cold wind of change was rustling the leaves. Although as much as ten years later the young Comte de la Rochefoucauld could still enthuse on a visit to Norfolk: 'As always I admired the way in which in all these little villages the houses are clean and have an appearance of cosiness in which ours in France are lacking . . .' and, as Arthur Bryant notes in *The Years of Endurance*: 'Houses were still cheap: a good cottage could be built for £50, and William and Dorothy Wordsworth were able to rent an ancient mansion in Somerset with a deer park for only £30 a year and live there handsomely on a legacy of £900', the cold wind was gaining in strength.

Before we move out of the eighteenth century into the nineteenth it may be interesting to examine further the flesh on the skeletal frame of the social structure and the sinews which held it all together. There was no middle class as we know it today – or rather middle classes, for nowadays there seem to be endless variations of status! Dickens got it more or less right when he wrote:

O let us love our occupations,
Bless the squire and his relations,
Live upon our daily rations,
And always know our proper stations.

The middle classes, then, had still to emerge from the Industrial Revolution and the consequent development of an urban society. Certainly there was a deal of what is now termed 'social upward mobility', with the wealthier farmers aspiring to squiredom even to the extent of keeping a tolerable wine cellar and riding out with the squire's hounds a couple of times a week; but by and large everyone knew their 'proper stations'.

The family fortunes of the aristocrat were followed with intense interest by everyone on his estate. If a child was born up at 'the big house' it was a matter for universal celebration. If he was the heir to the title, bonfires were lit on the hilltops, and when he came of age oxen would be roasted in the marketplace. When the holder of the title died, the tradesmen would shut up shop and line the streets as the tenants and trusted servants towed the bier to the last resting place.

This sympathy was not, however, by any means one-sided. The attitude of the big landlords towards their tenantry and employees was, by tradition, benign and paternal. They joined with them in country pursuits such as hunting and hawking, discussed their problems with them and called the most favoured ones by their first names. The wives of the squirearchy assumed the role of Lady Bountiful, visiting the sick and infirm, bearing with them well-meant gifts of calves' foot jelly. The parish poor might subsist at little above starvation level for most of the year, but on high days and holidays they would be invited to join in the mass celebrations at the squire's expense, when food and drink would be provided on a generous scale.

Charles Greville, writing after the turn of the century, gives us an entertaining account of the aged Lord Egremont holding open house at Petworth. Four thousand were asked,

but, as many more came, the old Peer could not endure that there should be
anybody hungering outside his gates, and he went out himself and ordered
the barriers to be taken down and admittance given to all. Gentlemen from
the neighbourhood carved for them, and waiters were provided from
among the peasantry. . . . Plum puddings and loaves were piled like cannon
balls and innumerable joints of boiled and roast beef were spread out.

Greville goes on to describe how the crowd swelled to ten thousand by
nightfall, when there was a firework display, and remarks how affecting
it was to see the host 'rejoicing in the diffusion of happiness and finding
keen gratification in relieving the distress and contributing to the
pleasures of the poor'.

The example set by the aristocracy was followed by the wealthy
landowners and gentry, which resulted in general benefit to the
countryside. In a class-conscious society, the number of servants kept
was important as an outward and visible sign of wealth. Likewise the
number of carriages and horses which were maintained, the spacious-
ness of the grounds which surrounded the mansion, and the lavish scale
of the local patronage were all of considerable moment in establishing
the standing of a family in its own and other people's eyes. The Duke of
Devonshire of the day who had the reputation of being a modest,
retiring man not much given to ostentation, employed a household staff
of 180 to look after the comfort of his person at Chatsworth, and in an
average week had five bullocks and fifteen sheep from his estate killed to
feed them.

The structure of the whole landed society is best viewed as a triangle,
with the dukes on a pedestal above the peerage; below them came the
baronets and knights, and below them again the lesser gentry, with the
freeholders forming a broad base. There are no very accurate figures of
the numbers of any but the very top category. The best guide is
probably the eighteenth-century statistician Gregory King, who put
the number of baronets and knights at 1,400 and the number of the
families of the lesser gentry at 15,000. All the landowners together
owned three-quarters of the cultivated land – all but the common land –
and controlled a quarter of the national income, so that, although the
interests of the larger and smaller landowners were not always conjoint,
they represented easily the most powerful section of the community.

Of course, each category of landowner was not nearly as distinct as
cold statistics tend to suggest. Some families of long lineage and great
territorial importance had no family title to support them – like the
Wyndhams of Wiltshire, the Chaplins of Lincolnshire, the Constables
of Yorkshire and the Cliftons of Lancashire, whose good luck it was to
own the land on which Blackpool was built. It was, of course, inevitable

that many of the smaller landowners who styled themselves as gentry were, either through bad management or through living above their means, crumbling on the brink of financial ruin and scarcely able to keep up their social pretensions with the more prosperous yeoman farmers. It was only in the very top echelons that there was no blurring of the social edges.

Because the ownership of land carried with it so much economic and political power, and so much social prestige, everyone was concerned with adding to what he already had, whilst the emerging rich merchant class strove to break into what was virtually a closed shop. There was very little land for sale, so that adding to the family estates by judicious marriages became a major preoccupation of the landowners. Batteries of lawyers found lucrative employment in arranging the complicated details of entails and settlements and dowries. Few families were prepared to accept the simple solution of the Earl of Southampton of the day, whose misfortune it was to have no male heir but only three daughters. In *The Russells of Bloomsbury* Gladys Scott Thompson describes the situation:

> Neither argument nor discussion had apparently been entered into. The Earl of Southampton, in his will, had merely desired his trustees to divide the properties into three parts, one for each of his daughters; or, if any one of those daughters was dead, then her share was to go to her children. He had expressed no wish as to how the lands were to be divided, nor how, when divided, they should be apportioned. But someone, whether a trustee or a daughter, had had a scheme. The estates being divided, according to the rentals, as equally as might be into three parts, the decision as to which part should go to which daughter had been left to the ancient biblical method of casting lots.
>
> That this was the procedure adopted is revealed in a note left by the second sister, Rachel. She says nothing of the manner in which the lots were drawn – nor even whether the three sisters met for the purpose. But on the outer sheet of a statement which is really a particular of the property which was to be her share is written in her own hand:
>> 'Valuation delivered to me by trustees 1668; the estates being at that time valued and divided into 3 parts.
>> My sister Noel, my sister Northumberland and myself cast lots.
>> Mine was:
>> The manors of Stratton Micheldever, etc, in Hampshire:
>> Southampton House and the manors of Bloomsbury and St Giles in Middlesex.
>> My father Thomas, Earl of Southampton, died 14 May, 1667.'
> So was decided the fate of a great estate.

Thus one sister brought further lands to the already land-rich Dukes of

Northumberland, whilst Rachel herself acquired the whole of Bloomsbury, as yet almost entirely undeveloped but destined to become the
crown jewel of the great estates of the Russells of Woburn Abbey. The
third sister, Noel's, portion founded the dynasty of the Montagus of
Beaulieu. The preoccupation of the great landowners not only with the
preservation of their estates but also with increasing them so that their
heirs might enjoy an even greater inheritance relied very largely on the
making of advantageous marriages.

There can be little doubt that the breaking up of the great
Southampton estates would not have happened in the way that it did
had the Earl been blessed with a male heir. The rule of primogeniture,
whereby an estate is left in its entirety to the eldest male heir to the
exclusion of any other issue is, of course, not a rule at all. Anyone is
entitled to leave his estate (subject to certain strictures) as he wishes.
Just the same, for the great landowner not to abide by the rules in this
respect would have been unthinkable.

As a precaution against any such catastrophe in future generations it
became the custom to entail estates, which placed a legal obligation on
the inheritor not to dispose of the estate after his death other than to a
specified line of descent, which down the years has led to some very odd
inheritances indeed. Cattle hands from the great Australian Outback,
South African gold prospectors or even American businessmen in Wall
Street have been uprooted to take over some vast, unheated castle
surrounded by bleak acres of moorland which they scarcely knew
existed.

Even in the best organized of families, this playing at the marriage
game must include an element of luck. In the traditional marriage
equation, ancient lineage counted very often for more than wealth, so
that the older established families found it easier to replenish the family
coffers in each generation by marrying heiresses, while the *parvenu*
families frequently impoverished themselves in obtaining suitable
alliances for their daughters. At the end of the eighteenth century we
find Lord Sefton's adviser advocating that his son, Lord Molyneux, be
the means of rescuing the family fortunes and clearing off a debt of
£40,000.

> To marry a fine brought up Lady with little or no fortune would be to hurt
> the Estate. By the Estate he has a right to expect a large sum with a Lady,
> not to look for less than £60,000 . . . *many* a great and rich banker would be
> glad to offer to give his daughter that fortune for her advancement and
> dignity (vide Messrs Child), or many a rich heiress to a large estate of good
> family would also be glad of the offer.*

* Lancashire CRO, Sefton MSS, DDM 11/63.1791.

There are many examples of how great estates were forged in the matrimonial chamber, like the elevation of the erstwhile minor West Country family of Russell to the Dukedom of Bedford, but there can be surely no more striking example than that provided by the equally obscure family of Gower from Sittenham in Yorkshire. Thomas Gower was knighted by James I and married twice. His first wife was the daughter of the Howards of Naworth Castle, and his second the daughter of a Sir John Leveson. A complicated succession followed by which the Gowers eventually became heirs to all the Leveson estates in Staffordshire and took the name of Leveson-Gower.

The first Leveson-Gower married a daughter of the Earl of Bath. It did not at first seem to be a particularly brilliant match until the lady was predeceased by her nephew, the last Earl of Bath, and became co-heiress to the very considerable Bath lands. Her son married the daughter of the wealthy Duke of Rutland, and in recognition of the growing importance of the family was made Baron Gower. His son married the daughter of the Duke of Kingston, and a daughter of this marriage married the Duke of Bedford. The second Lord Gower had the dubious distinction of being both President of the Jacobite Society immediately before the '45 Rebellion and serving at the same time in the Hanoverian Cabinet. He took the right political decision at the time of the Rebellion and raised a regiment for King George to fight his erstwhile colleagues, for which he was rewarded by being made Viscount Trentham and the first Earl Gower.

His son married the daughter of Scroop, first Duke of Bridgewater, who was in turn descended from Brandon, Duke of Suffolk, and Mary Tudor, which entitled the family to quarter the royal arms. He was also advanced in the aristocracy and became the first Marquis of Stafford. His son eclipsed all his forebears in the marriage stakes by gaining the hand of Elizabeth, Countess of Sutherland, the only surviving child of the seventeenth Earl of Sutherland, which was the oldest title in Britain and brought with it half a county. She had been left an orphan at the age of two, and her right to the lands was disputed both by the Sutherlands of Forse and the Gordons of Gordonstoun. Her claim was upheld, which made her one of the most eligible heiresses in the kingdom. Soon after the marriage, the Duke of Bridgewater died and all his great estates were inherited by the Leveson-Gowers, which made them the largest landowners in the country – a position they quickly improved upon by purchasing the other half of Sutherland from Lord Reay, the head of the Clan Mackay. This vast accretion of landed wealth was recognized when the second Marquis was created first Duke of Sutherland in 1883. Thus in four generations the Gower family had risen from mere knighthood to a Dukedom, and were probably connected by marriage with more aristocratic families than any other.

Nor did their success in the marriage market end there. The second Duke married the daughter of the Earl of Carlisle, and the three daughters of the marriage each married a duke – Argyll, Westminster and Leinster. The third Duke married the Countess of Cromartie, who also held the titles of Viscountess Tarbat and Baroness MacLeod and brought with her a large slice of Ross. Thus Bateman shows in *Great Landowners in Great Britain and Ireland*, the family landholdings in 1878 as:

	Acres
Sutherland	1,176,454
Ross	149,999
Shropshire	17,495
Staffordshire	12,744
Yorkshire	1,853
Buckinghamshire	1

The total, 1,358,546 acres, was over 2,000 square miles and more than a quarter of the area of Wales.

At the same time the descendants of Sir Thomas Gower of Sittenham were in possession of no fewer than eight separate peerages: Sutherland, Argyll, Leinster, Westminster, Ellesmere, Granville, Cromartie and Blantyre. It is little wonder that they were known in the nineteenth century as the 'lucky Gowers'.

Whilst advantageous marriage has played by far the greater part in the preservation of the big estates, political manoeuvring has also played an important role. The last substantial grants of land for taking the correct political view – or, rather, 'backing the right side' – were made when William of Orange assumed the English throne in 1689, but the repercussions continued all through the following century and well into the next. A case which illustrates the very essence of the political aspect is the *cause célèbre* which in the second half of the eighteenth century brought the two powerful houses of Portland and Lowther into conflict. That one of the parties in the dispute should have been the third Duke of Portland, whose ancestor had been one of the more extravagantly rewarded of William of Orange's *parvenus*, and the other the heir to one of the most ancient lineages in the kingdom, only added piquancy to the bitter dispute.

Of the two protagonists, the third Duke of Portland was by far the more important, certainly politically. He was to hold in turn the offices of Lord Lieutenant of Ireland, First Lord of the Treasury, and Secretary for the Home Department. Not only was he himself a Duke, but he was related by strong ties to another powerful ducal family, the Devonshires. His opponent was a very different kettle of fish. He was Sir James Lowther of Lowther Hall in the county of Cumberland. Lowther was a man of driving ambition who held a seat in the House of Commons, but really preferred the role of puppeteer to active personal participation. At one time he controlled no fewer than nine seats in the Commons, known as Lowther's Ninepins. One of his nominees was his erstwhile secretary William Pitt, for whom he secured the seat of Appleby.

The Duke of Portland was almost as active as Sir James in manipulating parliamentary seats. He controlled the two Wigan seats and made a determined attempt to return his own candidate for Cullington, near Southampton, where he had estates. Unsuccessful, he turned his attention to Cumberland where he also held land – and Cumberland was regarded by Sir James as his own exclusive territory. The result might have been just another struggle between great landlords of differing political colour, but the Duke had greatly underestimated his opponent.

Part of William of Orange's grant to the Dutch Bentinck family who became Dukes of Portland was the honour of Penrith, which had been in the possession of Catherine of Braganza, Charles II's widow. When she died, in 1705, the Portlands took possession of her lands which were considered to include the Forest of Inglewood and the Socage of Carlisle. The right to enjoy them remained undisputed until the third Duke decided to use them as the basis of his bid for political power against Sir James Lowther. He put two candidates in the field at Carlisle, one of whom was his brother, Lord Edward Bentinck, and two candidates up for the county, Henry Curwen and Henry Fletcher, who stood against Sir Joseph Pennington and 'Wicked Jimmy' himself. It was a direct attack against Lowther's omnipotence, and a serious one, for it soon became apparent that Portland commanded considerable support in his struggle against what many of the freemen regarded as Lowther's tyranny.

It was at this stage that Sir James played his master stroke, which was to raise the election out of the category of a local contest and make it one of the most hotly debated of the century. He struck at the very foundation of his opponent's power – his land. On 9 July 1767 he presented a memorandum to the Treasury which alleged that the Duke had no right whatsoever to the Forest of Inglewood and the Socage of Carlisle, which formed the greater part of his estate. He made his plea on two grounds: firstly that the lands had not been included in the original gift, and secondly that the King had anyway exceeded his rights in granting Crown lands to a subject in perpetuity. He maintained that they could not be granted for more than ninety-nine years or for more than three generations, and that in this case the three generations had already been expended. It was a bold stroke, but Sir James went even further, for he petitioned that Portland's leasehold should at once be revoked and granted to himself instead.

The Chancellor of the Exchequer at the time of the presenting of the memorandum was Charles Townshend. Horace Walpole gave it as his opinion that, 'rash and thoughtless' as Townshend was, 'he would at once have recognised the dangers of permitting an application to go forward, which, however well it might be justified in law, had a most glaring partisan motive'. Unfortunately for Portland, not only was Lowther's case thoroughly justified at law but Townshend was succeeded by Lord North before he could give his decision, and Lord North found no difficulty in finding for Sir James. Within a few months the Lords of the Treasury formally ordered the transfer of the lands to Lowther.

The degree to which this dispute had been elevated from a parochial squabble to the realm of power politics and personalities is easier to understand when it is realized that the First Minister of the Government was none other than William Pitt the Elder, once one of Lowther's Ninepins and now elevated to the dignity of Lord Chatham. At the time of the dispute an election seemed imminent. Lord Chatham had relinquished his political power in all but name and, shutting himself in a darkened room, left it to his puppets, first Charles Townshend and, on his death, Lord North, to oppose the bid for power of the Rockinghamites.

In the eyes of the aristocracy the transfer of the land to Lowther was, of course, a dreadful decision with far-reaching implications. Many of them held their lands on similar royal grants, and this meant that a political opponent with a little antiquarian zeal could not only knock them out of the political ring but deprive them of what they had considered to be their inalienable birthright. Nor did the decision arouse only the big landlords. Every freeholder in England felt that his property was endangered. The Rockinghamites made it a main plank of their political platform in the elections of 1768, and so great was the anti-Lowther feeling in his own county that all four of Portland's candidates were swept to power.*

* Sir James Lowther was actually returned by two votes for the seat of Penrith, but his election had been so blatantly manipulated that, on petition of a number of freeholders, the motion that he had been lawfully elected was overturned and Henry Fletcher named in his stead.

When the new Parliament met, one of the first measures to be introduced by the Opposition was a bill for the protection of private property. Introduced by Sir George Savile, its purpose was to give a subject who, for a period of sixty years, had enjoyed uninterrupted possession of lands granted by the Crown, the right to possession in perpetuity. The bill was passed at once by an overwhelming majority. The landowners had closed their ranks.

Unfortunately for Portland the new Act was not retrospective, so he still remained bereft of his Cumberland estates. He entered into a series of costly law actions, which lasted for ten years. In the end he succeeded, but by that time Sir James himself had joined the Rockinghamites and their political differences had been resolved. Sir James had had his fun and the cost to him had been a mere fleabite out of his income, which was said to be in the region of £200,000 a year. The affair nearly broke Portland financially, and shortly afterwards he sold the disputed land to his brother-in-law, the fifth Duke of Devonshire.

There is an interesting footnote to this history of struggle for landed power. Fifty years later the Reverend Benjamin Newton, a Yorkshire vicar of some distinction, thought it worth recording in his diary for July 1818 of a visit to the Lake District:

> My landlord told me Mr Curwen [the descendant of Lord Portland's elected candidate] would have joined Lord Morpeth to stand for Cumberland against the Lowthers, who seemed more disliked here than in Westmoreland but that Lord Morpeth would not join Mr Curwen; the expense of turning out the Lowthers would have been at least £50,000 if it has succeeded at last. . . . At last? It would appear very much a case of *plus ça change*, to have been *plus c'est la même chose*!

The incomes of the landlords in their varying degrees are hard to assess. Indeed, even if they could be quoted with any accuracy the actual figures would have little significance. The important point was that to be a great landlord was to be above financial worry, and to own land was all on the side of the 'haves' as opposed to the 'have-nots'.

The idyllic picture of the sons of honest toil homeward bound at the close of day to a picturebook cottage with roses round the door was far from the reality. Whilst the eighteenth century was largely typified by the rich becoming richer, the poor were becoming poorer. Those who worked the land were often so desperate that they were driven to stealing food from the pigs it was their job to tend. The one-room huts in which they existed were made of mud and straw, and their staple diet was meal boiled up into a porridge with a chaw of bacon or any other scraps which were to hand. The children were brought up to drink beer, which was both cheap and plentiful, and infinitely preferable to the water which was all too often a carrier of disease. They were put to work from a very early age, although in much more healthy conditions than were later to be experienced in the dreadful city slums which were one of the evils of the Industrial Revolution. They were generally employed for a few pence to stop cattle and sheep from straying, or stationed by a road gate in the hope of earning a penny tip from the occasional traveller.

A thrifty labourer earning between £6 and £7 a year might save enough to get married. If he could start married life with a potato patch, a cow or a flock of geese which he could graze on the common land, or even a few hives of bees, he was reckoned a good marriage prospect. As late as 1823 it was estimated that it took only £31 a year to maintain a labourer's family – £20 for food, £3 for rent and £8 for clothing – but it was not easy to earn such a sum from working the land, and there were many who had to attempt the impossible by living wholly or in part on parish relief. At the same time, Creevey the eighteenth-century diarist, reports that Lord Durham had earned for himself the nickname of 'King Jog' from his expressed opinion that 'one can jog along on £40,000 a year'.

The disparity in standards of living between the lowest and the highest, penury on the one hand and affluence on the other, the monopoly of privilege and power in the hands of so few at the expense of so many, was the sort of situation from which one might have expected revolution to have stemmed. By 1750 revolution was indeed on the way; it was not, however, to be a revolution of men against their masters. It was to be a revolution of ideas which was led from the top, and which was to last right up to the present day. Its first effect was to make the land-rich even richer, but at the same time it was to sow the seeds which were to result in the destruction of what the rich strove to preserve.

Although land in the early eighteenth century was all-important, it did not necessarily of itself bring great wealth. This was undoubtedly in part due to the fact that many of the big estates were poorly administered and this was often a deliberate policy. There were two main reasons why a landlord did not always attempt to extract an economical rent from his tenants, or encourage them with financial grants to make their land more productive. The first was simply that his love of sport led him to prefer that much of his land should remain in an uncultivated state. It was long believed that too much cultivation was inimical to hawking and to the rapidly developing sport of fox hunting, so that a farmer who worked his land in a way which provided the best sport for his landlord could expect to be relieved of the responsibility of paying too much rent.

The second reason was that the politically conscious landlords were not above courting popularity amongst their tenants. It was on them that they relied for support at the hustings, and a reputation for benignity in the matter of arrears of rents or concessions in reducing rents in hard times went a long way towards achieving this. In the rich lands of Rutland in the mid-eighteenth century, the rents to the Manners family averaged only a niggardly 3s 10d an acre, and the accumulated arrears in rents on the Chirk Castle estate of the Myddletons amounted to a disastrous £4,941 on a gross annual rental of £2,854.* Arthur Young, the great protagonist of the enclosures and a leader in the Agricultural Revolution, was indignant at the failure of the landlords to claim a realistic rent for their acres, in order to earn, as he wrote, 'an extra-low bow and scrape from the tenantry and engage their franchise'. Thomas Stone, another agricultural expert of the times, went so far as to declare that the absentee landlord with expensive tastes to provide for was a benefactor to his estates.

> The extravagant son of White's was worth ten times more to his country than the gentleman of regulation and moderation; his rents fly with the dice; down he comes into the country and raises to the utmost. No farmers will agree for a rent that they cannot pay . . . the consequence is that his estate is let at its highest value; this is but another word for good husbandry, for that which is bad will not pay great rents.**

For good landlords or bad, however, the early years of the eighteenth century were not a period which brought fat profit from the land. The population explosion was not yet under way and, though the methods used were inefficient, there was still more food being produced than the country needed. The estates round London and other large population centres could, it was true, find a ready enough market for their products, but in the more remote parts many farmers would have been unable to carry on if they had been saddled with higher rentals and avaricious landlords. Indeed, most landlords could not have survived unless they had had other strings to their bows.

It is a matter for some surprise that there still remain families of considerable antiquity who have preserved their estates down to the present day purely by the solid virtues of good management and the best aspects of feudalism. Nor would it be going too far to state that there are none where, in one generation or another, the future of an estate and the continuity of family ownership has not been put at risk by the indiscretions or negligence of one or more in the line of succession.

* Chirk Castle MSS 9945.
**Thomas Stone, *An Essay in Agriculture*, 1785; this passage quoted by G. E. Mingay in *English Landed Society in the Eighteenth Century*, 1962.

The preservation of an estate from generation to generation has aptly
been described as rather like riding a bicycle. Any sudden imbalance
in the forward progress of the machine can so easily result in a
wobble, and failure to correct the wobble in time can have disastrous
results.

Although indulging in trade was considered to put a man outside the
social pale, the great landlords themselves had highly developed
commercial instincts, and were not slow to avail themselves of the
opportunities offered by landownership. Long before the Grosvenors
contracted a fortuitous marriage which brought them a farm on the
outskirts of London, on which much of the present-day West End was
to be built, they were making rich profits from their lead mines in
Cheshire. There were few large estates which could not raise money
from the sale of timber, particularly during times of war, and many
others which drew sizeable incomes from lime and brick kilns, slate and
stone quarries, and from royalties on the coal, iron, tin and lead mines
which were excavated on their land. Coal in particular was to bring
immense wealth to the landlords as the appetite of industrial Britain
developed. Of the aristocratic families surviving today who owe much
of their wealth to coal, names like Durham, Northumberland,
Lonsdale, Dudley, Portland, Fitzwilliam and Rutland are obvious
examples. There were many others of lesser degree.

There was another way in which the lot of an aristocratic landowner
was made easier: the concept that the state had a duty to support its
aristocracy in adversity. The ownership of land was considered by
tradition to be necessary for the support of an hereditary title. To be
promoted to the aristocratic club presupposed that the candidate had
the necessary lands. On the rare occasions when a promotion was made
for merit, it was accompanied by a grant of appropriate magnificence.
Thus when John Churchill was elevated to Duke of Marlborough by a
grateful nation he added to his £10,000 a year as Commander-in-Chief a
parliamentary pension of £5,000 a year and the gift of large estates in
Oxfordshire on which Blenheim Palace was built for him. Lord Nelson
received the Trafalgar estate and a pension in perpetuity of £5,000 a
year (abolished by Attlee's Government of 1945). Others who earned
merit promotions were not always so fortunate. Admiral Rodney, for
example, was granted in addition to his peerage only a state pension of
£300 for himself and his heirs in perpetuity. However, the general
principle that a peer must have the means to support his title has been
maintained until quite recent times. As late as 1919, Field Marshal
Haig refused to accept an earldom for his services in the First World
War 'unless an adequate grant was made to enable a suitable position
to be maintained'. When he became Earl Haig, a gift of £100,000

accompanied the honour. None of the Second World War leaders, however, received more than life pensions.

Peers who, through extravagance, ill-considered marriages or misfortune, found themselves in straitened circumstances, could usually rely on the state to grant them a pension; but, more important, there were numerous offices of profit under the Crown for which they qualified and for which there was keen competition. The most sought-after prize was the Paymastership, which was worth £4,000 a year to the holder but in addition gave him unlimited opportunity to feather his nest in other ways. The Paymaster could, for example, demand commissions for negotiating foreign loans, and could reserve for himself the interest on money held for the pay of the troops. Henry Fox, father of the Whig statesman Charles James Fox, made his fortune in this way and became the first Lord Holland. Even more notable, or notorious, was James Brydges, the son of an obscure Herefordshire gentleman, who made himself immensely wealthy and became the first Duke of Chandos entirely through ingratiating himself into higher and higher Government office until he too achieved the lucrative Paymastership.

The Black Book lists some of the more exotic offices held by members of the peerage at that time. Earl Bathurst, for example, was one of the most assiduous collectors of sinecures: in addition to his modest £1,500 a year as one of the eleven Commissioners for Affairs of India, he collected £23,117 a year as Teller of the Exchequer. Viscount Cathcart drew £14,000 a year as Lord Vice-Admiral of Scotland. The Hon. R. D. Kenyon held the office of Filazer and Exigenter at £4,986 a year, while the Earl and Countess of Westmeath earned a total of £4,460 from their posts as Auditors of the Imprest Accounts and Clerk of the Hanaper. The range of offices available, from Paymaster of the Marines to Prothonotary in the Court of the King's Bench in Ireland, was as long as it was varied and, by and large, these offices were the prerogative of the heads of noble families or their eldest sons. The rule of primogeniture applied equally to any perquisites which might be going. Younger sons were thrown out of the nest to make their own way in the Army or the Church or as administrators of the rapidly growing Empire. Unfair though the practice might have seemed to the younger sons who suffered from it, there is no doubt that it was the single most important factor in preserving the great landed estates from generation to generation. On the Continent, where estates were divided up amongst the sons of each generation, estates became subdivided to the point of extinction.

By the middle of the eighteenth century, however, there were other influences at work which were to bring about an erosion of the landed omnipotence.

2
The Nineteenth Century

The significance of the Agricultural Revolution is sometimes overlooked by historians in their preoccupation with the Industrial Revolution. The Agricultural Revolution, however, played a vital role in making its industrial counterpart possible, and the landowners played a decisive part in both.

Medical science was taking great strides forward, with the result that infant mortality was drastically reduced and people were living longer. After centuries of remaining more or less static, the population figures took a great leap forward; instead of there being an overproduction of food, it became a matter of pressing importance that more food should be produced.

Up to the beginning of the nineteenth century, whilst the ownership of land had brought with it great social prestige and political power, the activities of the estate owners had not been designed to produce great wealth from agriculture. There had, of course, been exceptions to this general rule. Amongst the more notable was Lord Ashburnham who, like the Duke of Portland, had received his title and a grant of preferential Crown lands in Sussex from William of Orange. Unlike the Duke of Portland, he was less concerned with high office and political power than with the old-fashioned virtues of good husbandry. He managed his estates with such care and attention to detail that he added considerably to his fortune, which enabled him in turn to lend money on mortgage at a high rate of interest to his less provident fellow landowners. This, coupled with the necessary flair in the marriage market, enabled the Ashburnhams within a few generations to become one of the most land-important families in the country.

There were others, like the Duke of Bridgewater, who employed his creative genius in the development of the inland waterways system. His canals anticipated by over half a century the great revolution brought about by the railways, and gave impetus to the changing scene by making it possible, for the first time, for goods (and particularly His Grace's own coal) to be moved cheaply from one area to another.

However, by far the majority of landowners had been content to occupy themselves in improving their sporting rights and surrounding their parks with impressive walls. They were not intellectually decadent, for they showed themselves willing to patronize the arts, filling their houses with fine pictures and furniture and setting great store by their knowledge of the classics, but a study of improved methods of agriculture had not generally come into their repertoire.

It might be claimed with some justice that the apathy of the landowners towards agricultural improvement had sprung from the lack of financial incentive. But when the time came they were quick to see the opportunity offered them by a vastly increasing home market for their produce, and set about cashing in on the situation with the utmost vigour. It was a revolution which started at the top and spread rapidly downwards through the echelons of lesser landowners, who were ever eager to copy anything which was the fashion, particularly if it was also profitable. It was altogether a topsy-turvy revolution, for it was the dispossessed who resisted it most fiercely and the rich who forced it upon them.

The keystone of the Agricultural Revolution was the introduction of the system of enclosure. For centuries the countryman without land of his own had had the right to use the great areas of common land. It was, however, a most uneconomic system. Not only was the common land grossly over-grazed, which resulted in the raising of sub-standard stock, but cultivation of crops on common land was virtually impossible. There were no fences to preserve such crops from the depredations of cattle, horses and sheep, and there was no capital available to plant them even if they had been a practical proposition. The more far-seeing and ambitious landowners were not slow to see that, if greater productivity was to be achieved, the common lands could not be allowed to survive. That they represented the inalienable right of the people presented little difficulty in a country where all power was vested in the hands of the landowners. All that was required was for a private Act to be passed through Parliament which gave the right to enclose particular areas of common land. These private Acts were expensive processes: only those who had the means to pay the heavy legal costs involved, as well as to stand the additional expense of fencing, could benefit – the total bill could come to as much as £10 an acre. Thus the well-established landowners became bigger, while the poor man lost not only his right to the common land, but his cow or his flock of geese as well, as he now had nowhere to graze them. Even Arthur Young, the chief advocate of enclosures, admitted the unfair way in which it operated. 'By nineteen out of twenty Enclosure Bills,' he declared, 'the poor are injured and most grossly.'

Unfair or not, however, the enclosures were a necessary step in raising productivity. They were also to have a far-reaching sociological effect. By depriving the poorest classes of what little rights they had, the Acts made them entirely dependent on the bigger landowners for their livelihood. Nor was it only the very poor who were affected. Many cottagers and small yeoman farmers found it uneconomic to carry on and were forced to sell up their smallholdings. A whole new class of agricultural labourers was created, who were forced to try to wrest a living from employers who, in view of the keen competition for jobs, needed to offer only the barest wages. If the weather was too wet to work in the fields, they could lay off their hands, so that great numbers were obliged to eke out a miserable existence between poorly paid employment and inadequate parish relief. While agricultural prices boomed, thousands of poor families were being driven from their cottages to seek employment in the growing industrial towns. There, crowded together in the evil slums, and forced, in order to exist, to send their children to work in the sweat factories, they discovered that they had exchanged one impossibly hard way of life for an even more impossible one. In a country beginning to burst at the seams with money, the plight of the very poor was desperate indeed.

For the big landowners, however, conditions had never been more prosperous. In his book *English Landed Society in the Eighteenth Century*, G. E. Mingay quotes the following figures as a rough guide to the incomes of the various categories of landowners at the end of the eighteenth century:

	No. of families	Range of income	% of land owned
I Great landlords	400	£5,000–50,000	20–25
II Gentry			
(a) Wealthy	700–800	£3,000–5,000	
(b) Squires	3,000–4,000	£1,000–3,000	
(c) Gentlemen	10,000–20,000	£300–1,000	50–60
III Freeholders			
(a) Better sort	25,000	£150–700	
(b) Lesser sort	75,000	£30–300	15–20

The Acts of Enclosure destroyed a centuries-old way of life for the countryman. Superficially it might be claimed that they destroyed much of what was admired and envied by visitors from abroad – the contented lot of those of the peasantry lucky enough to be part of the largely benign feudalism which was practised by the majority of the great estate owners. But to criticize the Acts on this account is to ignore the many benefits to the countryside as a whole which were to stem from what many social commentators of the time were to describe as the grossest form of discrimination of the rich against the poor – a process as despicable as the Clearances in the Scottish Highlands which still evoke so much bitterness almost two hundred years later. Today even the most biased must regard the Agricultural Revolution, of which the Acts of Enclosure were an integral part, as being, along with the Industrial Revolution, a necessary catharsis in the process of making Britain great.

The countryside on the whole presented a barren appearance. There were great acreages of open land with only the walled demesnes of the squirearchy to break the monotony. The new possessors of what had once been common land soon discovered that the quickest and most economic method of fencing off their property was the planting of hedges, with the result that the whole landscape took on a new look. Most of the hedges which beautify the countryside today were planted between 1760 and 1840, when the process of enclosure was virtually completed. The land developers also planted trees at intervals along their hedgerows, for timber was in even shorter supply and could provide a profitable source of revenue. Coppices were planted, to be cut young to make gates and for other agricultural uses, and hardwoods grown to provide timber for all manner of new needs. Landlords encouraged – and indeed sometimes forced – their tenants to plant uneconomically broad hedgerows as cover for game. It was sometimes a sore bone of contention with the tenants that they should be forced to surrender fertile land in this way, but it certainly had the effect of making the aspect more pleasing. Cobbett went further, and claimed that the wooded areas actually brought more prosperity to the labourer. Of the great grasslands of Hampshire, he wrote:

> These countries have one great drawback; the poor day-labourers suffer from want of fuel and have nothing but their bare pay. For these reasons they are greatly worse off than those of the woodland countries; it is really surprising what a difference there is between the faces that you see here and the round, red faces that you see in the wealds and forests, particularly in Sussex, where the labourers will have a meat pudding of some sort or other; and where they will have a fire to sit by in winter.

The 'meat pudding' to which he refers was, of course, derived from the game which the landlords sought to preserve in their woodlands, for poaching was a source of food to the countryman as well as of money, as there was a ready market for game.

Hand in hand with the Acts of Enclosure came a revolution in agricultural practice. Men like Coke of Norfolk, later to become Earl of Leicester, led the way. He showed by practical demonstration how the sandy soil of his Norfolk lands could be made to grow crops and rear stock. Before his day it was said that there were two rabbits fighting for every blade of grass on his estates at Holkham. By the time he died, his tenants were amongst the most prosperous in England. 'It has been objected against me,' he once said, 'that my tenants live too much like gentlemen, driving their own curricles, perhaps, and drinking their port every day. I am proud to have such tenantry, and heartily wish that instead of drinking their port they could afford to drink their claret and champagne every day.'

Where Coke led, many followed. The fifth Duke of Bedford travelled to Holland to study drainage, and returned to introduce the Dutch system in reclaiming the fenlands. Lord Townshend became known as 'Turnip' Townshend because of his pioneering of that crop. The fourth Duke of Richmond and the fourth Duke of Portland were both noted agriculturalists. So were the Lords Althorp, Egremont and Rockingham.

The enthusiasm with which the aristocracy and the great land-owners in general greeted the Agricultural Revolution was not, as we have seen, shared by the population who earned their living from the land, and the newly rich farmers and lesser squirearchy did little to alleviate the situation. The irascible Cobbett, biased against the landowners as he undoubtedly was, gives a convincing picture, confirmed by other writers of the times, of the class which had been made rich by the agricultural boom during the Napoleonic Wars:

> The English farmer has, of late years, become a totally different character. A fox-hunting horse; polished boots; a spanking trot to market; a 'get out of the way or by G–d I'll ride over you' to every poor devil on the road; wine at his dinner; a servant (and sometimes in *Livery*) to wait at table; a painted lady for a wife; sons aping the young squires and lords; a house crammed with sofas, pianos and all sorts of fooleries.

It will be noted that Cobbett's spleen was largely directed against the *nouveaux riches*. It is ever the lot of those who accumulate new money to be despised for their pretensions, both by those socially superior who resent their presumption and by those from whose ranks they have so recently risen.

That such fortunes should be gained in time of war is, in particular, galling. The army which marched over Westminster Bridge with George III and his two sons at its head one cold February day in 1793, an event which marked the start of the Napoleonic Wars, was largely made up of peasant refugees from agricultural poverty, enlisted to fight the King's enemies. Few could have foreseen that the campaign, culminating in the Battle of Waterloo, was to last for almost a quarter of a century. As Arthur Bryant remarks in *The Years of Endurance*, the youngest survivor of those who marched that day would be in his forties when he returned.

In that quarter-century a whole cycle of agricultural prosperity had gone by, leaving behind it the high tide of the newly prosperous and the inevitable agricultural depression which had left the poor poorer than ever. Driven to the limits of endurance by poverty there is no doubt that bloody revolution was in the thoughts of the English labourers during the agricultural depression which succeeded the prosperous war years. Whilst the large landowners were in a position to survive cycles of prosperity and depression, the labourer could not buffer himself. Deprived of his small measure of independence by the enclosures, he could only rely on parish relief – which was in any case well below subsistence level – if he was put out of work. As the farmer's reaction to a price recession was usually to cut down on his workers, the farm labourer's existence was a precarious one indeed. In the spring of 1816 there had been rioting in East Anglia, with bands of hungry labourers roaming the countryside, setting fire to barns and stacks, demanding higher wages and cheaper food and bearing banners inscribed 'Bread or Blood'. The winter which followed was one of the worst in memory. The potato crop failed, wet weather prevented much of the wheat crop being harvested, and sheep died by the thousand. The condition of the poor was indescribable. Many emigrated, and still more fled to the towns and left the land for ever.

As the years of depression followed one another, many of the smaller landowners also began to suffer seriously. Tenants were unable to pay the rents of more prosperous years and, in many cases, had to give up altogether, and the bottom dropped out of the land market. Great tracts of newly enclosed land went out of cultivation. In Norfolk, land to the value of £1½ million was up for sale and found no buyers.

Once more, only on the really big estates did the unfortunate find any hope of being sheltered from the universal misfortune. The Duke of Portland introduced a sliding scale for rents which was tied to the price of wheat, and the Duke of Bridgewater made it a rule never to refuse an applicant for work; as a result he had at one time eight hundred men employed on his estate at Ashridge.

Not all the great landlords, however, were so benign. With all the political power in their hands, they took little effective action to relieve rural distress. Parliament appointed a succession of Select Committees which achieved little or nothing. The Whigs pressed for an end to the misuse of political power and to the nepotism which was rife, yet when they gained power in 1830 they cynically ignored their promises. Indeed, Lord Grey, the Whig Prime Minister, set a new standard of nepotism by rewarding three sons-in-law and two brothers-in-law with political office.

Agricultural unrest went hand in hand with the demand for reform generated in the urban areas, and reached its peak with the Swing Riots of 1829–30. The winter of 1829 was even more disastrous than that of 1816, and the country was in a worse condition to endure it. Matters were further aggravated by the introduction of the newly invented threshing machine. For many the only regular work available during the winter months had been the laborious threshing by flail, for which they earned a pittance sufficient to enable them to survive. The new threshing machine represented a direct threat to men already at the point of desperation, and they were prepared to take direct action to defeat it. Rioting broke out afresh in Norfolk and rapidly spread to other parts of the country. The chief objective of the rioters was to break up the threshing machines, but their violence extended in other directions. There were new outbreaks of stack burning – although it was a crime which was punishable by hanging – and unpopular farmers were attacked by the gangs which roamed the countryside.

The outbreaks were so numerous and conformed so much to a pattern that it was generally believed that they were centrally organized. Farmers received illiterate notes threatening reprisals if they bought the hated machines, which usually ended with the melodramatic phrase: 'Beware the fatel dagger', and were signed 'Swing'. Whether such a person as Swing ever existed is not known. In the minds of the terrorized farmers, however, he was very real indeed. He was generally spoken of as Captain Swing, and it was a name which became feared throughout the land.

The bigger landowners, however, were not so easily frightened, and they possessed the means of defending themselves. They had the power of appointment of the magistrates, who were backed by an Act of 1827 which for agricultural sabotage laid down vicious penalties, ranging from seven years' transportation to hanging. These were powers which they did not hesitate to use. On 2 December 1830 Lord Brougham, the Lord Chancellor and a newcomer to the ranks of the landowners, rose to address the House of Lords: 'Within a few days from the time I am addressing your Lordships, the sword of justice shall be unsheathed to smite, if it be necessary, with a firm and vigorous hand, the rebel against the law.'

Brougham set up a series of Special Commissions to try the rioters, and the Commissioners were not unwilling to demonstrate their fitness for the task. At Winchester they convicted 101 prisoners, of whom six were condemned to be hanged and the rest transported for life. At Salisbury two men were sentenced to death, and 154, some of them no more than boys, were transported. Commissions followed at Aylesbury, Dorchester, Reading and Abingdon. By the time the task was done 457 men had been transported, 400 more imprisoned and nine lives had been forfeited. The total would have been higher had not public indignation forced the magistrates to temper the severity of their sentences. There was in fact a great deal of public sympathy for the rioters, who were, after all, only asking for a wage of 2s 6d a day, which should not have been outside the means of most farmers, hard-pressed though they were themselves.

'The scenes of distress in and about the jail are most terrible,' wrote the *Times* correspondent after the Winchester Commission.

> The number of men who are to be torn from their homes and connections is so great that there is scarcely a hamlet in the country into which anguish and tribulation have not entered. Wives, sisters, mothers, children, beset the gates daily, and the governor of the jail informs me that the scenes he is obliged to witness at the time of locking up the prison are truly heart breaking.

The Commissions had the effect of quelling the rioting, but they remain one of the blackest marks in the history of agricultural development. 'After the law had been thus vindicated,' wrote W. H. Hudson,

> it was generally agreed to raise the wages by one shilling. But by and by, when the anxiety had died out, when it was found that the men were more submissive than they had ever been . . . they cut off the extra shilling and wages were what they had been – seven shillings a week for a hard working seasoned labourer with a family to keep. . . . But there were no more risings.

Everywhere in England there was change. In the hundred years between 1750 and 1850, the period roughly covered by the enclosures, not only did the whole appearance of the countryside alter out of all recognition but the whole structure of society became subject to fresh influences, which resulted in the emerging of a new order. On the face of things the old aristocracy remained as powerful as before, but there were cracks which were beginning to show.

One manifestation of change was in the greatly increased number of the aristocracy. It was a tradition which had been started by William Pitt the Younger and which was to continue with ever-increasing impetus up to the present day. A story quoted by the diarist G. W. E. Russell tells of Pitt being approached by Mr Smith, a wealthy banker, who asked him if he could be given the privilege of driving his carriage through the Horse Guards as a short cut from his London house to his Office in the City. 'It is beyond my powers,' replied Pitt. 'But I can make you an Irish Peer.' Next day Mr Smith was created Lord Carrington.

Pitt, who for political reasons was anxious to extend the peerage, still accepted the dictum that a peer should have the land to support his dignity. The increasingly complex problems posed by a rapidly expanding economy called for a wider range of skills in government than had hitherto been available amongst the traditional aristocracy. Pitt found them amongst the leaders of the legal profession and the City, although Disraeli's criticism that 'he caught them in the alleys of Lombard Street and clutched them from the counting-houses of Cornhill' is a typically colourful piece of exaggeration. Both Peter Thellusson, whom he created Lord Rendlesham, and Robert Smith were country gentlemen more than bankers by the time of their elevation, and of the fifty-odd new peerages which Pitt created many were drawn from the Diplomatic Corps and the armed forces. Just the same, it was a big step towards the dilution of the ancient nobility and opened the door for the later creation of industrial peers.

Other changes were afoot. In 1830 the Manchester–Liverpool railway opened for business. 'England's gift to the world' was viewed with mixed feelings by the aristocracy and gentry. Landowners who had experienced the benefits brought by the Duke of Bridgewater's canal system were for the most part quick to see the advantage of the new invention. Others forecast nothing but disaster to the countryside. For the most part the objectors were concerned that the noisy and smelly monsters would pass close to their mansions and destroy the amenities for ever. Others, like the Duke of Cleveland, successfully petitioned against the railway on the grounds that it would cut through their foxhunting coverts and ruin their sport. There was another body of opinion which held that the provision of quick and comfortable transport to London would result in landowners spending too much of their time in the metropolis, to the detriment of their estates.

It was typical of the vested interests which opposed the railways, however, that even the most diehard reactionaries could be softened by the prospect of profit. The impoverished Marquis of Ailesbury, for example, made a great show of his desire to preserve the amenities of Savernake Forest and his mansion, Tottenham Park. At the same time he privately agreed with the London, Bristol and South Wales Direct Railway for a main line through Marlborough, with a station on his land, in consideration of a payment of £30,000. It was never built, but when the Great Western came along with an offer of £14,000 for seventy acres of land and a further £5,000 for disturbing his peace at Tottenham, he again agreed with alacrity. Many other landowners managed to sell their land for three or four times its agricultural value by threatening opposition.

On the other hand many other landowners enthusiastically embraced the idea of the railways. Sir James Graham, with an eye to the advantages accruing to his agricultural estate of Netherby, in easier transportation of his produce, declared himself to be 'on velvet' when he knew that three lines would be crossing his lands. Landowners with industrial interests poured their own money into branch lines which would connect their coalfields and other interests with main lines, while the Lords Committee investigated ways of enabling further landowners to raise money for the purpose.

Within ten years even the most cautious had been convinced of the new prosperity brought by the railways, which would enable them to charge higher rents from their tenants. While the coaching and posting business withered and died, the railways spread their tentacles throughout the country at a headlong rate. Thirteen years after the first line was opened, the Bull and Mouth, the most famous of the great London coaching yards, was up for sale, with only three of its once proud fleet of seventy coaches surviving. Yet another great revolution had taken place.

By the middle of the nineteenth century the whole aspect of land-ownership had changed. When the great Reform Bill of 1832 had been passed, the Lord Bathurst of the day had cut off his pigtail, the mark of a superior courtier, saying, 'Ichabod, for the Glory is departed.' It was not the glory which had departed but, with the abolition of many of the pocket boroughs, the power that was diminished. The Duke of Wellington deplored the passing of the bill on the grounds that it would drive gentlemen out of politics. As a traditionalist he could foresee nothing but disaster if politics became the preoccupation of any but the landed gentleman; although unfounded, this was a view for which there was considerable support well into the twentieth century. Reluctant as the Duke might have been to admit it, however, there was already a new power in the land which had been making its influence increasingly felt. It was no longer the landowners first and the rest nowhere. The Industrial Revolution was bursting into flower, bringing with it a new aristocracy of money.

Of all the fortunes which were being made, the greatest and the most 'respectable' were those of the bankers. Socially they stood nearer to the landowners than any other category of the *nouveaux riches*. Many had close business relationships with the aristocracy, and others were linked by marriage. By the middle of the century the tendency for the big estates to grow even bigger had started to slow down. The spectacular advancement of families like the Leveson-Gowers and the Granvilles* in the eighteenth century was never to be repeated.

With the amassing of so many new fortunes, the line of demarcation between the landed and the industrial interest became more distinct. Although many landowners benefited from the Industrial Revolution

* The Granvilles had linked the fortunes of the families of Temple, Nugent and Chandos, to be created first Marquesses then Dukes of Buckingham.

and were involved in it to a greater or lesser degree, the tendency more and more was for them to represent the agricultural interest and to regard themselves as the *ancien régime*, superior to and remote from the vulgar cries of the marketplace. Those who did not, like the Butes who busied themselves building the docks in Cardiff, or the Lonsdales who virtually created the mining town of Whitehaven, became immensely wealthy. Families who found themselves in possession of the lands on which the new industrial cities were being built, found wealth thrust upon them. Thus the Norfolks grew rich as Sheffield developed, the Derbys profited from the growth of Liverpool; and the Westminsters, the Cadogans, the Portlands and the Bedfords, to name only a few, found that the new streets of London were indeed paved with gold.

Some families were less fortunate. Perhaps the most spectacular misfortune was the one which overtook the Duke of Buckingham, whose estates amounted to well over 50,000 acres but who had so over-reached himself financially that he no longer had the means of holding them together. It is often said that the huge sales of land which were forced on the second Duke between 1844 and 1857 – a total of nearly 46,000 acres – were the result of his being honoured by a visit from Queen Victoria when she stayed for a few days with her retinue at his seat, Stowe Park. It was certainly an honour which only the very rich could afford, and, it is alleged, the Duke put a brave face on it by dressing the bailiff's men as butlers for the occasion – a device which did not amuse the Queen when she found out about it. It is more likely, however, that he was the victim of his own poor administration and of the bad agricultural years. Known as the 'Farmer's Friend', he knew more about the theory of agriculture than the practice.

Whatever the cause, the sale of such large acreages was almost unprecedented, and it offered an opportunity for rich men without estates to acquire them and join the envied ranks of the landowners. The most ready buyers were the bankers. The Duke's Aston Clinton estate at Tring was bought by Sir Anthony de Rothschild, and the neighbouring estate of Aston Abbots was acquired by Samuel Jones Lloyd of the Manchester banking firm of William Jones, Lloyd and Co., later better known as the Westminster Bank. Samuel Lloyd was subsequently created Lord Overstone. In Hampshire another banker, Alexander Baring, was busy carving out an estate. Earlier he had paid the heirs of the last Duke of Bolton £64,200 for the Itchen Stoke estate. Now he added to it the Duke of Buckingham's lands at Itchen Abbas. Baring was an avid acquirer of land. 'Property is very essential to me,' he wrote, 'and I am therefore a very willing purchaser.' He received the aristocratic kiss when he was made Lord Ashburton.

Another noted banker who was an enthusiastic purchaser of land was Henry Drummond of the Charing Cross Bank. After a great deal of buying and selling he finished up with the Albury estate in Surrey. He had no male heir, and the estates subsequently passed into the hands of the Dukes of Northumberland when Drummond's daughter married Algernon George Percy, who was to become the sixth Duke. The weight of great wealth was, not for the first time, prising open the door to social acceptance, which was, indeed, still the trump card in the hand of the landowners.

The financial return on investment in the land had become small by comparison with that on investment in industry, and was no longer the main source of material wealth. In many cases landowners who invested money in land improvements could only regard it, at best, as a rescue operation for their tenants and hope that their heirs would reap richer rewards. It is to their credit that so many of them continued to pour money into drainage schemes and other agricultural operations when many of their contemporaries were spending their money more recklessly. To quote one example, the Duke of Northumberland spent substantially over £200,000 in the 1850s, which resulted in an improvement of a mere 1.4 per cent in his rent roll.

Interest on invested capital in safe industrial stock brought between 3½ and 4½ per cent, 'without adding a penny for labour'. A landowner would be lucky if he got half that return for his investment. Even worse, his investment was likely to deteriorate steadily in the shape of falling rentals, arrears and even empty farms if he did not put money out on drainage schemes and other improvements to keep pace with the technical advances in farming methods. The Duke of Cleveland, the Marquis of Bath and Lord Sidmouth between them poured £3,450,000 into their estates, with very little better immediate result than had been achieved by the Duke of Northumberland. By and large the great landlords, and particularly those with incomes from sources other than their lands, were willing to make these financial investments in their estates. Amongst the smaller estates owned by the gentry there were many who were either unwilling or unable to follow suit, with the result that the properties ceased in time to provide any sort of return and had to be sold.

Yet in spite of the poor return from land investment, there was no diminution in its desirability. To own land was still the passport to the achievement of social ambitions, and there were few industrialists who were not anxious to gain admittance to the ranks of the socially privileged. For the few who succeeded there were many who failed.

Britain, and particularly the Midlands of England, was becoming the workshop of Europe, but as Professor Asa Briggs has remarked, there is no greater gap in our social history than the lack of biographical material on the worthies who led the Industrial Revolution. While the population of towns like Manchester, Sheffield, Newcastle and Wigan quadrupled, and more and more mills and factories were built, surrounded by their satellite slums, the big manufacturing families remained as anonymous as their factory chimneys. In the scramble for industrial wealth there was initially little time for gracious living, and even less for considerations of civic pride. It was only in 1866 that the Corporation of Manchester, which now rivalled London in size, sought to acquire a site to erect a Town Hall. Ten years later the town of Crewe, which, with the coming of the railways, had grown from a village to a township of 24,000, could boast only 170 water closets.

Today there is only a scattering of soot-blackened statues standing outside public buildings to commemorate the nineteenth-century industrialists. A few were knighted, a few more became members of Parliament, but by and large all of them have sunk without trace. They owned no estates to hand down from generation to generation, and in the competitive atmosphere of commercialism it was very often a case of 'from clogs to clogs in three generations'.

The ephemeral nature of the industrial fortunes was in part due to the periodical financial crises which overtook the expanding economy. In 1793 there had been a crisis so serious that the Liverpool Corporation had had to print its own banknotes to carry its traders through. Another crisis occurred in 1810, when it was estimated that half the traders in the kingdom were forced into bankruptcy. In 1837 the shortage of money was so grave that the great international shipping and banking house of Brown, Shipley & Co. was only saved from ruin by a loan of almost £2 million from the Bank of England, and many smaller banks put up the shutters. In 1866 the country ran out of money again. There was simply not enough to go round to finance all the speculation which was taking place in new building, railways and factories. On 10 May the great banking firm of Overend and Gurney collapsed, over-extended to the extent of £19 million. In the panic that followed several other banks failed, the finance for some of the new railway companies dried up and thousands of families were ruined.

These were vicissitudes of fortune from which, by and large, the landowners held themselves aloof. In the eighteenth century many had plunged into active participation in mining the minerals found under their land. In the nineteenth century it became the tendency more and more for their successors to withdraw. Certainly the mine-owning families continued to enjoy great incomes from their mines, but this came in the form of royalties rather than earned profits. On the River Tyne, for example, it was estimated that by 1830 only five of the forty-one collieries were worked by their proprietors; on the River Wear only three were. All over the country speculators and adventurers were taking over the mineral rights of the great landowners in return for royalties. One of the few who retained control was the industrialist Earl of Durham. It proved a chancy business: in 1873 his mines made the astonishing profit of £380,000; three years later they showed a loss of £65,000.

The growth of the big cities was probably the most fertile source of wealth to the landowners in the second half of the nineteenth century. Their incomes from property developments are hard to assess, but they must have been enormous, and they have, of course, continued to grow. The Duke of Portland, who owned most of Soho and Marylebone, estimated his rents in 1844 at £50,000 a year, compared with a mere £4,000 a year fifty years earlier. The Grosvenors and the Russells owned even more valuable property in London. Outside London, the Duke of Devonshire owned most of Eastbourne, the Cliftons owned Blackpool, the Norfolks Sheffield, the Seftons and the Derbys Liverpool, and so on. An inquiry into urban holdings held in 1886 discovered that out of 261 provincial towns, 69 were largely owned by the great landlords, and 34 by families from the gentry. The changing shape of Britain was bringing into being a new type of landowner – or rather creating a new type from the old. The decline in the value of agricultural investment meant that the purely agricultural estates were finding it very hard to survive, and only those landowners who had an industrial source of income remained impregnably wealthy. Of the agriculturists, a few tried to mend their broken financial fences by investment in one or other of the many wild speculative enterprises which were constantly being proposed.

One of the schemes which excited widespread interest was investment in the cattle pastures of the American Middle West. Travellers brought back tales of fantastic profit to be made from the golden prairies, and cattle fever swept the country. It was even rumoured that Queen Victoria herself had invested in a herd of longhorns. At one time it was estimated that British capital controlled well over 20 million acres of American cattle country. One of the most enthusiastic supporters of the scheme was the Earl of Aylesford, who sold his English estates and invested in a 40,000-acre ranch in Texas. Unfortunately the first severe winter wiped out most of his stock. He was so hard hit that after paying for thirty horses, thirteen dogs and five servants he had no money left to buy more cattle. Known by his neighbours as 'the Jedge', he gained local fame by his performance with the whisky bottle. He would always open a new bottle for any cowboy who cared to drop in, and, as one of them reported, 'He didn't stop at one neither, I've been to the ranch many times to stay all night and woke in the morning to find the bottles lying around as thick as fleas, the boys two deep on the floor snorin' like mad buffaloes and the Jedge with a bottle in each hand over in the corner.' Aylesford was not the only English aristocrat to suffer. The Rosslyns, the Rodneys and the Lonsdales all invested in one grandiose scheme in Wyoming, but lost 80,000 head of cattle in the blizzards of 1878 and sold up. There were many similar stories.

Perhaps the oddest phenomenon which affected the decline of the landed interest in the nineteenth century was the willingness of some of the aristocrats to officiate at the funeral of their own power. Whilst there were many like the Duke of Northumberland, the Duke of Richmond and Sir James Graham of Netherby, who strove mightily to preserve the traditional power of the landowners by improved methods of land management in an age when the aristocratic influence was steadily declining, there were others who actively supported democratic agitation. One notable example was the seventh Duke of Bedford, who inherited not only one of the greatest landed estates of the century but also a brand of Whiggery which seemed to contradict his position in society. It was a characteristic which each generation of the Russell family had shown to a greater or lesser degree. In the early days they had stood against oppression by the Crown, and, in the person of Lord John Russell, the family creed of supporting liberty took the form of championing the idea of government by the people instead of by the aristocracy. He supported the Reform Bill, holding that the Tory boroughmongers were the root of all evil. Just the same, this did not stop him being one of the most assiduous of all the Russells in his efforts to maintain and improve the family inheritance. He provides a striking contrast to his neighbour the Duke of Buckingham, who had the cannon from his yacht brought ashore in order to fight Reform. Yet it was the Buckingham estates which crumbled and the Bedfords who went on from strength to strength.

Disraeli was a strong supporter of the view that the future prosperity of the country still lay with the landed interest. His respect for their institutions was such that, when he was raised to the peerage, he borrowed money to acquire an estate so that he could join their ranks. Over the execution of Disraeli's policies, however, we find the ranks of the big landowners divided. In 1886 the Marquis of Bath was writing: 'Of all the delusions which have infected English political life in my time, there is none which seems to be more wonderful than the belief that genuine conservatism has any proper home in a party which was formed by Disraeli and is now led by Salisbury.' Twenty years earlier his aunt had written to him: 'We can never have a united party as long as Dizzy is at the head of it.'

Yet Disraeli had no difficulty finding aristocratic allies. It was one of the most powerful of them all, Lord Derby, who presided over the passing of the Second Reform Bill which had the effect of increasing the franchise; this caused the equally powerful Duke of Northumberland to remark that Derby and Disraeli 'have let the mob in on us'. Just the same, for most of the century the landed interest continued to provide a majority in the House of Commons. It was only in the Parliament of 1885 that the commercial interest for the first time predominated. In scarcely fifty years an unreformed House of Commons which sat almost entirely in the landed interest had not only repealed measures like the Corn Laws, which they had earlier passed for their own protection, but they had reformed themselves to a point where by the abolition of the rotten boroughs they were deprived of the very electoral powers which they had seemed to hold so absolute. That such a transformation should have taken place without bloodshed is remarkable, to say the least.

3

The Aristocratic Grip Relaxes

During the eighteenth and nineteenth centuries, as we have seen in chapters 1 and 2, large landowners and the aristocracy were more or less synonymous. By the end of the nineteenth century and the beginning of the twentieth, however, matters were far less clear-cut. It would not be entirely true to say that it was a period which marked a sort of *Götterdämmerung* of the English landowner-aristocrat, for in many ways his power was as great as ever. It was rather that the herd instinct for self-preservation which had ever been strong in the species now indicated that the time was ripe to assume some protective colouring. The reasons were simple enough. In the first place the enormous fortunes made during the Industrial Revolution had led to a 'new aristocracy' proliferating at an alarming rate. The great industrialists, without the normal qualification of great landed wealth, were knocking at the gates of entrenched power and could no longer be denied.

By the turn of the century the sluice gates had been well and truly opened, and the aristocracy could no longer claim to be a small, exclusive club bound together by a community of interest. Between 1886 and 1914, 246 new titles came into being, of which scarcely a quarter were drawn from the heads of old landowning families. It is an accurate indication of how far the ownership of land had declined in importance in relation to the muscle of the industrialists. Certainly professional men, diplomats, colonial administrators and retired generals and admirals were received into the peerage in increasing measure, but it was the new industrialists who had the larger slice of the cake. Although contemptuously referred to as 'the beerage' because of the large number of ennobled brewers (Ardilaun, Iveagh, Hindlip, Burton and Marchamley), the new promotions actually covered a wide field of activity. For example, W. H. Smith of bookstall fame became Lord Hambledon; Mr Cunliffe-Lister, who became Lord Masham, was a woollen merchant; the new Lord Cheylesmore was in silk; and Lord Armstrong of Cragside was an armaments king. The net was cast even wider with the inclusion of men like Donald Smith of the Hudson's Bay Company. When he became Lord Strathcona his wife could claim the distinction of being the first Red Indian to become a peeress. 'For political services' became the most commonly used description to justify an ennoblement, but a significant number of new peers were drawn from industrialists who had played no part in politics: for example, men like Lord Inverclyde of the Cunard Shipping Line, and

North American industrialists like Mount Stephen and Strathcona. But the most important political offices, and the court appointment, continued to be the perquisite of the old landowning classes. With the exception of Disraeli, it was not until Asquith* formed his administration in 1908 that the tradition that the Prime Minister should also be a landowner was finally broken.

The dilution of the peerage had the effect of changing the public image of the aristocracy, but it did little to reduce the social advantages still to be gained from owning land. Although to own land was no longer a condition of ennoblement, many of the new peers were sufficiently traditionalist to acquire estates to support their new dignity and to adopt the way of life of the traditional landowning classes. Most were content to acquire a county seat with a thousand acres or so to support it, but a few were both wealthy and enthusiastic enough to invest heavily in land. By the time of his death, Lord Armstrong of Cragside owned 16,000 acres in Northumberland, and Lord Masham had invested almost £1 million in acquiring the Jervaulx Abbey estate from the Marquis of Ailesbury, and Swinton Park, another large Yorkshire estate. Sir Edward Guinness conducted a long and earnest search for a suitable property to justify his transition from Irish brewer to English landowner, before finally purchasing Elveden Hall and 17,000 acres in Suffolk from HH the Maharajah Duleep-Singh. It was precisely this sort of thing which sent the established aristocracy scuttling for cover.

It had been certain ever since the failure to get the Limitation of the Peerage Bill through Parliament in the early eighteenth century that a gradual increase in the numbers of the aristocracy was inevitable. Pitt the Younger, in particular, had accelerated the rate of promotion to the peerage for political advantage but, like Disraeli after him, had been a devoted believer in identifying such promotions with the landed interest. Perhaps the worst aspect of the new avalanche of promotions from the point of view of the Old Guard was not only the eagerness but the ability of the newly ennobled to identify themselves in the public eye with what was undoubtedly the most exclusive club in the world. That the Guinnesses, the Rothschilds and many others of the newly wealthy could, in one single generation, by sheer force of money outdo families who over centuries had zealously collected all that was best in furniture, pictures and possessions, who had patronized down the years the finest artists, landscape gardeners and furniture makers and so built a heritage in order that future generations should bow the knee

---

* Campbell-Bannerman (Prime Minister 1905–8), although a Glasgow businessman, came from a landowning family.

and tug the forelock in deference to their elitism, was an intolerable erosion of their traditional position. For them elitism spelt power. Now the whole carefully balanced structure was in peril. In short the bicycle had developed a wobble and it was seriously threatening to get out of control.

The reaction of the *ancien régime* was to distance themselves as far as possible from *les nouveaux*. Thus as the plump figure of Queen Victoria in her widow's weeds shrank ever further into the shadows, appearing with increasing reluctance on public occasions, the old aristocracy also put up the barricades. Suddenly it was not done to appear in fine clothes and to strut upon the stage. To plead poverty and imminent ruin became the fashion. To 'be in trade' was to be placed right outside the social pale, the very height of vulgarity. It was to bring about a sort of social revolution which has continued to echo on into the present day.

Although there was a social change afoot, the last quarter of the nineteenth century saw a phenomenon which struck much more deeply at the entrenched position of the landowners. This was the great agricultural depression which lasted from 1873 to 1896, and was much more serious than any which had gone before. The root cause of the depression was the vast increase in imported foodstuffs which brought prices tumbling down. Wheat poured in from the American prairies and from Canada, Australia and the Argentine, and as a result the price of English wheat dropped from 56s a quarter in 1871 to 22s 10d a quarter by 1894. Improved refrigeration techniques made the importation of cheap beef from the Argentine a practical proposition and Danish eggs and bacon were invading the British market for the first time.

The effect of this long depression on the landowners was, in some cases, catastrophic. The hardest hit were the corn regions of the Home Counties and the sheep and corn farmers of the Wiltshire Downs. In those areas where bankrupt tenants left their farms, it was almost impossible to replace them. Rents fell sharply, so that by 1896 they were on average 4 per cent below what they had been in 1873. Farmers who reared stock were not so badly hit, but even in the stock-rearing counties rents were down by from 10 to 20 per cent.

The agricultural depression had struck very deeply at the entrenched position of the landowners. One of the main effects had been to widen the gap between the really rich landowners and the smaller estates. Northumberland, Derby, Lonsdale and Westminster were buffered from financial misfortune by mineral royalties or by their urban properties. Others, like the Duke of Buckingham, Lord Verulam and the already financially crippled Marquis of Ailesbury, found themselves faced with the necessity of trying to sell part of their land at a time when there were few willing purchasers. As the President of the Surveyors stated in 1883: 'We shall probably look in vain for any great increase in the demand for land, and the market will be filled, as at present, with anxious owners, of whose offers to sell no heed is taken by capitalists.' With the need for greater economy in their style of living, many of the old established landowners sought to sell off outlying parts of their estates. Faced with the prospect of moving out of their over-large country houses, which were becoming ever more expensive to maintain, or selling part of their lands, most chose the latter course. This policy, continuing from one generation to the next, inevitably resulted in the family lands being so diminished that, even with the return of great prosperity to the land, they no longer had sufficient acres to support their way of life. The number of landless mansions which dot the countryside today are evidence of the economic vortex in which many landowning families found themselves as a result of the great agricultural depression.

The lesser gentry and squirearchy were the hardest hit of all. Many found themselves in the uncomfortable position of being able neither to maintain their lands nor to sell them, and were forced to live off their rapidly diminishing capital. This resulted in a further weakening of the traditional role of the landowner as a power in local affairs. Harassed by financial worries, he withdrew more and more into his shell, and much of the influence he had once held passed into the hands of the wealthier tradesmen.

There is some piquancy in the fact that it was only those landowners with other sources of substantial income who were equipped to weather the storm, although to suggest that they were in any way 'engaged in trade', like the newcomers against whom they had so firmly shut their gates, would have amounted to sacrilege. By the turn of the century the power of the landowners had been severely shaken, but it was by no means at an end. In fact it was to enjoy what F. M. L. Thompson calls an Indian summer until the catastrophe of the First World War.

Before progressing with the history of landownership into more modern times, it is interesting to examine who the large private landowners were in the second half of the nineteenth century. That accurate figures are available is due to the efforts of the fifteenth Earl of Derby. He sponsored the idea of compiling the *Return of Owners of Land*, commonly known as the New Domesday Survey, which made its appearance in 1873. Lord Derby's object in pressing for this survey was to combat the often-quoted criticism by land reformists that the greater part of the British Isles was in the hands of a mere 30,000 individuals. Intended as a political weapon which would place landownership in a

more favourable light, it proved to be quite the opposite. Although the
Return listed a million names as owning land to some degree – even if it
was only a back garden – the most striking point that it demonstrated
was that four-fifths of the kingdom was in the hands of only 7,000
people.

It only requires the most superficial study of the *Return* to discover
that the number of acres owned by individuals bore almost no relation
to the amount of income derived from them. There were sixteen people
in England and Scotland shown to be receiving more than £100,000 a
year in rentals:

Incomes of £100,000 or more	*Acres*	*£ rental*
Marquis of Anglesey	25,505	107,361
Duke of Bedford	87,507	141,577
Duke of Buccleuch	458,739	216,026
Marquis of Bute	116,668	231,421
Lord Calthorpe	6,470	122,628
Earl of Derby	56,598	150,326
Duke of Devonshire	198,665	180,990
Earl of Dudley	25,554	123,176
Earl Fitzwilliam	115,743	138,801
Marquis of Londonderry	50,323	100,118
Duke of Norfolk	44,638	269,698
Duke of Northumberland	186,297	176,048
Sir Lawrence Palk Bt	10,109	190,275
Duke of Portland	162,235	124,925
Sir John Ramsden Bt	72,448	175,631
Duke of Sutherland	1,358,546	141,679

The list is as interesting for those it excluded as for those who are
included. The terms of the *Return* were so vague as to allow the
traditional landowners to conceal their wealth while offering an
opportunity for New Money to boast. It makes no mention, for
example, of the Duke of Westminster, who was undoubtedly already
the richest man in the kingdom. His landed estates, however, only
amounted to 19,809 acres, at a rental of £37,776 – a sum which was
dwarfed by the ground rents of his London properties, which were not

shown on the *Return*. By the same token, neither Lord Calthorpe nor Sir Lawrence Palk could be regarded as really great landowners: in both cases ground rents from urban properties have been included. Calthorpe derived no less than £113,707 of his income from the lordship of the Manor of Edgbaston, Birmingham's fashionable suburb, and Palk owned the land on which Torquay was built. In the same way, Sir John Ramsden's income is inflated by ground rents on his West Riding estate, the Duke of Norfolk owned a large area of Sheffield, the Butes much of Cardiff and Anglesey, and Dudley parts of industrialized Staffordshire. The Duke of Bedford, on the other hand, does not include his urban rentals, which would have made his income return second only to Westminster.

A more valuable guide to the largest landowners as opposed to the richest is given on page 123, which lists everyone who owned over 100,000 acres. Of the thirty-five names listed, no fewer than twenty-five held their lands largely or exclusively in Scotland, where the rental returns were derisory compared with their English counterparts. Only the Duke of Buccleuch, with his rich border lands, could take his place amongst the really rich. The Earl (later Marquis) of Breadalbane, who could walk in a straight line for over a hundred miles without setting foot off his Perthshire estates, could show just over a quarter of Buccleuch's rental from almost the same number of acres. Even more impoverished by comparison were landowners like Sir Kenneth Mackenzie of Gairloch, whose 165,000-acre estate brought in scarcely £8,000.

The closing years of the nineteenth century and the first decade of the twentieth was a period of transition from one way of life to another, and the landowners reacted to it in different ways. There were many who, driven by financial necessity, withdrew more and more from public life, to become dubbed in a later era 'backwoodsmen'. Where it had been *de rigueur* earlier in the century to maintain an establishment in London, these men now dispensed with the idea, the practice of sending their sons on the Grand Tour of Europe fell into abeyance, and they withdrew more and more from involvement in national affairs, which had previously been one of their main preoccupations. Instead they struggled to maintain their estates on a profitable basis, and found their recreation in the traditional sports of the countryside.

There were others who reacted in quite a different way. With the end of the stifling respectability of the Victorian era in sight, and a new fashion for extravagant living on the way, many wealthy landowning families entered into the new spirit with zest. Ostentation was the order of the day as they vied with one another in the magnificence of their retinues, the opulence of their house parties, and the glitter of their entertainment during the London season.

Socially, where the Prince of Wales led many followed. The pattern set at Sandringham, of lavish shooting parties and gargantuan dinners followed by dancing or gambling, was reproduced in stately homes all over the country. The needs of tenant farmers took second place to the need to rear more and more pheasants or to provide a good line of country for foxhunting, and, out of season, many of the great houses remained untenanted while their owners followed the social round in London, Goodwood, Cowes, Paris or Biarritz, or enjoyed the increasingly fashionable sport of shooting grouse in Scotland. The fifth Earl of Lonsdale, whose ancestor had been 'Wicked Jimmy' Lowther and whose vast income came from his rich undersea mines at Whitehaven, kept two big steam yachts at Cowes, entertained more royally than royalty itself at his castle in Cumberland, and spent, it is alleged, £3,000 a year on cigars. That he should have been dubbed by Lord Ancaster, one of the Old Brigade, 'almost an Emperor but not quite a gentleman' would seem to say it all. It was, however, only a very small section of the old landowning aristocracy who joined in the merry-go-round.

Even after he ascended the throne, Edward VII's taste in friends was a catholic one. While many of the Old Brigade muttered behind their hands, he made much of his friendship with self-made men like Sir Ernest Cassel and Sir Thomas Lipton, whom, in spite of their great wealth, would otherwise have found it difficult to gain social acceptance. The Joels and Barnatos, who had left the East End of London a few years before to make vast fortunes in South Africa, returned to find the most exclusive doors open to them. Another South African pioneer, Sir Julius Wernher, bought the historic mansion and estate of Luton Hoo, and almost at once became a pillar of society.

The great landowning families with long political traditions, like the Cecils, the Cavendishes and the Churchills, still retained great prestige and wielded great power, but they mixed on equal terms with the new men of ability like Asquith, Chamberlain and Haldane. Even the great political hostesses like the Duchess of Sutherland and Lady Wimborne, the entree to whose soirees was sought after as much because they were exclusive as because of their brilliance, began to find competition from such newcomers as Margot Tennant (later Asquith), whose family fortunes were founded on soap. Oddly, too, Beatrice Webb, the heiress to a large industrial fortune, and her husband Sydney were received in the best houses in spite of their sponsorship of the Fabian Society, whose ideals might be said to strike at the very foundations of inherited wealth and privilege.

Even in the matter of marriage, the old-established families showed themselves to be more liberally minded than ever before. The turn of the century saw a spate of marriages between the aristocracy and the

stage. Within a few years three 'girls' from the old Holborn Casino –
Kate Cooke, Rose Wilson and Valerie Reece – became, respectively,
the Countess of Euston, Lady Verner and Lady Meux. The Marquis of
Headfort, the Earl of Orkney and Lord de Clifford married Gaiety
Girls, and the Marquis of Ailesbury married an actress called Dolly
Tester, who later ran off with the notorious Squire Abingdon.
Abingdon compensated the Marquis with a payment of £15,000, but
later abandoned Dolly to pursue Lillie Langtry. Events which a quarter
of a century earlier would have proved major scandals became reduced
to the proportions of nine-day wonders.

The business of advantageous marriages, however, still remained a
serious one, and an important means of preserving the great estates in a
changing world. There was any amount of new wealth anxious to
become associated with the old, and a completely new field opening up
in the increasing number of American heiresses in search of titled
husbands; and in the twentieth century, with such distinguished
examples as had been set by the Churchill family, the number of
Anglo–American marriages continued to grow.

Most of these manifestations of change were on the surface, but there
were others which went deeper. The great agricultural depression had
done much to shake the faith of the landowners in land as the be-all and
end-all of their existence. The evidence of the great fortunes being made
out of industry tempted even the most reactionary to look beyond their
park gates for a means of bolstering their falling incomes. Add to these
factors the return of an overwhelmingly strong Liberal Government in
1906, with its determined attacks on what was termed the 'land
monopoly', and the general unease which afflicted the established
landowners is simple to understand. For the first time, legislation gave
tenants the right to seek compensation from landowners for unreasonable disturbance. County Councils were given compulsory powers of
purchase for land to be used as smallholdings, and undeveloped land
became subject to duty.

During the nineteenth century it had been quite usual for aristocrats
to take seats on the boards of railway companies, but this was generally
as far as they allowed themselves to be drawn into industry. In the
greatest commercial nation in the world, commerce still remained
socially unacceptable. By the twentieth century, however, attitudes
had undergone a considerable change. It became a common practice
for landowners to sell off outlying parts of their estates and to invest the
money not only in Government stocks and bonds but in industrial
shares. The Cecils, for example, sold agricultural land in order to invest
in urban property, and the Duke of Portland spread his money into
such widely diverse interests as breweries, South African gold and

South American railways. When the Bute family sold the considerable part of Cardiff which they owned, they reinvested in property in Gibraltar and Tangier, as well as buying part of Madison Avenue in New York. The Duke of Bedford was not so long-sighted. When he sold Covent Garden for over £1 million he invested all the money in Russian bonds, which when finally redeemed in 1987 were worth more behind glass than cashed in. The third Earl of Verulam, on the other hand, saved the failing family fortunes by making a full-time career for himself as a businessman. By 1913, directors' fees alone accounted for over one-third of his income. The landowners were again showing their ability to change with the times, the better to preserve their heritage.

It is probably also true to say that there were many old-established landowning families who would have been only too happy to divest themselves of their estates if they could have found purchasers. That there were many who would have regretted the decision is suggested by the case of the Charlton family, who had owned their large Helseyside estate in Northumberland for over six hundred years. They put their land up for sale in 1887 but, finding no buyer, had no option but to retain it. That they are still in possession of it today is no doubt a matter of great satisfaction to them.

After the great agricultural depression the land market did not start to mend until a few years before the First World War, by which time the amount of land in the market was enormous. In 1913, for example, a total of 800,000 acres changed hands. Walter Long, a front-bench Conservative member who had sold off much of his Wiltshire estate three years earlier, had blamed his decision on the attitude of the Government towards large landowners, which, he claimed,

> compels all of us who are interested in land to most carefully consider our position [sic]. We who are owners have done our best to act as if in partnership with our tenants and have not been governed by purely mercenary considerations. A change, however, is coming over the scene, and those of us who do not possess other sources of income must regulate our affairs accordingly.

As F. M. L. Thompson remarks, Long may have been trying to make political capital out of what was primarily a financial decision, but his statement does reflect the unease which was widely felt amongst the landowning classes. With much of their political power dissipated, they looked fearfully to a future when they might be forced, by more and more radical legislation and increased taxation, to surrender their lands altogether.

Apart from the comparatively few instances when whole estates were transferred from one owner to another, there was a new tendency for tenant farmers to buy their own farms. Thus yet another process in the slow breaking up of the big estates had started. The Edwardian 'country house set', in fact, represented the last spurt of the flame before it went out altogether. By the time the country had emerged from the First World War, only the vestiges remained. As was remarked at the beginning of this chapter, there were still many landowners who played an active part in politics, but their number was to diminish rapidly. The day of the professional politician was at hand and the day of the amateur landowner was ending.

4
The Inter-war Years

The first decade of the twentieth century presented a gloomy picture indeed for the traditional landowning families. Certainly the First World War, as do all wars, brought temporary prosperity to the farmers and land sales fell to a trickle, but with the end of the conflict the prospect facing the estate owners was even bleaker than before. Taxation was becoming ever more onerous. In many cases death duties were making the sale of estates necessary. Even worse, the fearful sacrifice of life had left many estates without an heir, so that much of the point of preserving the old way of life had gone. As *The Times* put it:

> The sons are perhaps lying in far away graves . . . and the old people, knowing there is no son or near relative to keep up the old traditions, or so crippled by necessary taxation that they know that the boy will never be able to carry on after they have gone, take the irrevocable step.

By 1919 well over half a million acres were in the market, and in 1920 the figure was even greater. 'We all know it now,' announced *The Times*. 'England is changing hands.' It certainly seemed to be true. Even the greatest landowners were putting some of their estates on the market. The Duke of Rutland sold 28,000 acres of his Belvoir estate in 1920, and the transaction was hardly completed before he put his 12,500-acre Scarisbroke estate on the market. Other prominent sellers included the Dukes of Westminster and Beaufort, the Marquis of Bath and the Marquis of Northampton. The Duke of Northumberland sold his Stanwick estate in Yorkshire and the Albury estate in Surrey, and in 1921 *The Estates Gazette* announced that one quarter of England must have changed hands.

In many cases the estates were broken up and sold to the tenants, for it was seldom that a willing buyer was to be found for a whole block of land. In the ten years which followed the war, the percentage of owner-occupied land jumped from 11 per cent to 36 per cent. The yeomanry, which had shown a marked decrease in the nineteenth century, was making its appearance again. At the same time the various forces which had already been at work in blurring the edges of the reality of power in the governing of the country were not made any less clear-cut by the continued determination of the old aristocracy to distance themselves as far as possible from the new.

The enormous fortunes made during the First World War had been duly recognized by elevation to the House of Lords for more or less anyone prepared and able to pay for the privilege. Such peerages bore no particular political significance and were designed largely to fill Lloyd George's coffers, but they did tend to result in the withdrawal to the backwoods of some of the old landowning families with a tradition of being politically active. All the same, the House of Lords remained a strongly Conservative body. Even in the House of Commons, under Stanley Baldwin's administration of 1924–29 by far the greater number elected in the Conservative interest were in receipt of rentals in one form or another, and indeed fewer than fifty-three members were from old aristocratic families. It is also worth noting that, for those with political ambitions, to be of independent means meant that they might expect to be elected to Parliament about ten years earlier than their counterparts who had to work for a living; which meant in turn a better chance of rising to high political rank and power. The evidence of radical change was, however, to be seen on all sides.

This great transference of land heralded the appearance of a new figure on the scene – the land speculator. When the Marquis of Ailesbury sold 25,000 acres of Savernake, it was all bought by a speculator who at once sold it off by lots. More frequently the speculator made his appearance when there was urban property for sale. The town houses of the Grosvenors, the Lansdownes and Devonshires were pulled down and rebuilt as hotels, offices or clubs. By 1930 only four of the great houses remained in private hands – Apsley, Bridgewater, Holland and Londonderry. Today only Apsley House remains, where the Duke of Wellington still occupies a flat on the top floor of his mansion, which he has turned into a museum.

Apart from their town houses, landowners like Bedford, Portman and Southampton sold off considerable portions of their ground rents either to pay death duties or to retrench their positions. This was the great period of withdrawal, with estates getting smaller and smaller and the landowners' political influence in the national arena dwindling.

To add to their discomfort, the costs of labour and materials started to rise, without there being any compensating rise in rents. In the years immediately following the war, rents had risen to an average of 26s 5d an acre by 1921, and were maintained at around this figure until the 1930s, when they started to fall rapidly. By the time of the agricultural depression of the 1930s the national average was down to 21s, and in some areas, such as Norfolk, land was going begging. Many of the erstwhile tenants who had bought their own farms lived to regret it. They were unable to meet rising costs, and unprotected now by the umbrella of a liberally minded landowner, so farm bankruptcies became a common occurrence in the 1930s. Many farms would have remained unworked for lack of a tenant but for a great exodus of Scottish farmers from their native land. Accustomed to more rigorous conditions at home, many of them travelled south to take over the near derelict farms and managed by good husbandry to make them pay. It was their good luck that they had established themselves by the time the Second World War brought about another agricultural boom. Today, particularly in Norfolk and Wiltshire, farmers of Scottish origin are almost as commonly met with as their English counterparts.

The period between the wars might be regarded as the nadir of the landowners' fortunes. Increasingly deserted by the Conservative Party in whom they had put their faith, they were disillusioned by rising taxation and demoralized by the effects of the First World War. Their houses had grown too big for them and they could no longer afford the staff to run them. A few of the more fortunate were able to retreat to one wing and open the rest of their homes to the public at half a crown a time; others sought company directorships to bolster their falling incomes; but, for the most part, they did little to help themselves. It was as if they were living in the past and unable to adapt themselves to the changed conditions. The Hon. E. F. L. Wood (afterwards Lord Halifax), speaking in the House of Commons in 1924, forecast the changes that were on the way: 'Taking a view of British Agriculture . . . there is a silent revolution in progress. . . . We are, unless I mistake, witnessing the gradual disappearance of the old landowning class.'

In a sense the 'silent revolution' had already taken place, for the political importance of the landowners was dying away to a flicker; but even this flicker was capable of rousing the ire of the increasingly powerful Labour Party, to whom the old regime represented everything tyrannical and anti-progressive. Lady Londonderry, the last of the political hostesses, continued to give her soirees for the elite in her great chandeliered drawing room in Park Lane, which drew the fire of left-wing commentators like Claude Cockburn. He accused what he christened 'The Londonderry House Set' of political manipulation, but he was attacking the shadow rather than the substance. On the whole the landowners were more and more preoccupied with their own struggle for survival than with national affairs.

In defence of the general criticism of the landowners' ineptitudes in the years between the wars, it may be said that these were largely due to the hopelessness of the situation in which they found themselves. The agricultural depression precluded their farming their own lands, or doing other than hoping to survive on the low rentals they were being paid. As Captain H. Widnell, then agent for the 10,000-acre Beaulieu estate owned by Lord Montagu, puts it, in discussing the 1930s:

It was my greatest dread that a farm would fall vacant for which we should be unable to find a new tenant. We were so short of capital that we could not afford to take over a vacant farm even if it could be made to pay, which was doubtful. Instead we made what money we could out of cutting our coppices to supply the hazel wood industry, or felling trees on the natural regeneration plan.

In spite of the bucolic image which Stanley Baldwin liked to present to the electorate, he was the first to realize that his political fortune lay in wooing the industrial vote. While thousands of gallons of home-produced milk were being poured down the drain every day, and the price of meat and dairy produce slumped, the British farmer had to endure unrestricted competition from abroad, and even the indiscriminate dumping of foreign produce, because of the necessity of providing cheap food for the working man, while there were few voices raised to argue his plight in the House of Commons.

Nor did the estates which were supported largely by coal royalties find themselves in much better shape. By the end of the First World War the Duke of Northumberland, for example, had gross mineral royalties amounting to £82,450. By the time Mineral Rights Duty, Excess Mineral Rights Duty, income tax and supertax had taken their toll, this amount was reduced to £23,890: a very different picture from the relatively tax-free days of the previous century.

In political circles opinion had taken a full turn. The landowners were no longer regarded as a class whose interests must be protected; rather they were thought of as a source of revenue to be exploited to the full. Far from being recognized for their leadership of the Agricultural Revolution in Europe, they had acquired a public image created largely from the writings of Cobbett and the caricatures of the eighteenth- and nineteenth-century novelists, such as Henry Fielding's Squire Western or Thackeray's Sir Pitt Crawley. It was not an image that they were to find easy to shake off.

That the plight of the landowners did not attract any great public sympathy must also be put down to the fact that, on the face of things, they did not appear to need it. Although there were thousands of small landowners and yeoman farmers going through a period of real hardship, nothing had changed very much on the surface. The grouse moors of Scotland still attracted the very rich in August, there was still a much publicized London season, and foxhunting had become more fashionable than ever. All this provided an inexhaustible supply of ammunition for those who wanted to decry the inequality of privilege. That vast industrial fortunes were being made did not seem nearly as important as the fact that there was still a great deal of inherited wealth. Lord Lonsdale's yellow carriages may have disappeared from the scene, but there were still individuals with the money and inclination to cut a dash as country gentlemen. In spite of the effects of war in breaking down class barriers, there were still some who sought acceptance of their new wealth by the acquisition of land. In 1933 Mr Nall-Cain, the brewer, became Lord Brocket after purchasing Lord Melbourne's old seat, Brocket Hall in Hertfordshire; and there were several others financially able and anxious to adopt the way of life of the country gentlemen as an escape from the taint of commercialism. During the same period Lord Hillingdon, the banker, was said to have spent £200,000, during the ten years of his mastership of the Grafton, on hunting and racing.

Of all the activities of the countryside none was more widely criticized than hunting. The sport which Oscar Wilde described as 'the unspeakable in full pursuit of the uneatable' typified, for a large section of the urban population, everything that was wrong with the land-owners. Surtees' pen-picture of Lord Scamperdale – 'stumpy, clumsy and ugly' – who lived on tripe and cowheel in the steward's room of his country mansion, and never spent a penny on anyone or anything but foxhunting, was, for many people, the prototype of the landowning class. That a type of hard-riding, hard-drinking landowner such as Squire Mytton had once been part of the country scene is true, but he was the eccentric exception rather than the rule. By the end of the First World War it was already an out-of-date picture. In fact, the changes which had taken place in the hunting field were typical of the whole pattern of change over the past hundred years.

Until well into the nineteenth century hunting had been an activity controlled entirely – like everything else in the countryside – by the great landowners. They owned the packs of hounds to which they gave their names, and usually owned all the land over which the packs hunted. They paid the wages of all the hunt servants, and invited their friends to hunt with them, much as a landowner today might invite his guests to a shooting party. The land over which they hunted was largely unenclosed and uncultivated.

By the end of the century the picture had completely altered. Most of the packs had passed out of private ownership, so that anyone could hunt by paying a subscription, and the whole business had taken on social overtones far removed from the original conception. Young blades from London, out to cut a dash, took hunting boxes in the shires, paid their money and galloped enthusiastically – and not always considerately – over cultivated land, while the rural gentry, partic-ularly in the more accessible areas, took more and more of a back seat. The splendid turn-out of the more fashionable packs like the Quorn, the Whaddon Chase and the Grafton, and the hunt balls given to raise money, attracted a new social life from the towns to the countryside, enthusiastically supported by some and fiercely criticized by others. By the 1930s, however, foxhunting was completely unrepresentative of the countryside. Only a very few of the big landowners had remained personally involved. The Duke of Beaufort, Lord Fitzwilliam and Sir Watkin Williams Wynne still personally owned the packs which bore their names, while the Duke of Northumberland owned the Percy and Lord Yarborough the Brocklesby; but a hundred years earlier the list would have included most of the great names in the country.

It was not until the outbreak of the Second World War that the fortunes of the farmers, and consequently those of the landowners, started to improve. Land prices rose steadily, until by 1945 they stood higher than they had for seventy years. This was a very different situation from that which had obtained at the end of the First World War. A number of circumstances brought this about, the chief of which was the realization, by institutional investors as well as landowners, that to own land was likely to be the best hedge against inflation. With a new Labour Government in power with an overwhelming majority the political outlook was uncertain, and where uncertainty exists the most attractive refuge for investment capital is land. It was also realized that land in Britain was still cheaper than in almost any country in Europe. Many institutions were bound by statutory limitations to invest either in gilt-edged securities or in land, and the prospects for gilt-edged were dismal. Typical of this type of restricted investment were trust funds such as those held by the Oxford and Cambridge colleges, traditionally big investors in land, and similar bodies like the Company of Merchant Venturers. Between 1945 and 1950 many of the university colleges withdrew from gilt-edged and invested in land to a very considerable extent. Over the centuries the Merchant Venturers of Bristol had gradually given up their original role as Bristol wharfingers and shipowners and had become a body of trustees administering various charities. They were, for example, left £3,500,000 by the tobacco magnate H. O. Wills for the purpose of setting up a charity for old ladies suffering from incurable diseases. They decided in the postwar years that their best investment was in land. The big insurance companies also entered the land market, and so did were many others. In addition there were some large private investors, for whom there was the added atraction of relief from estate duty. Sir William (later Lord) Rootes bought a large estate in Scotland, as did insurance chief Sir Brian Mountain.

The boom in land prices, as a result of all this activity, is not in itself sufficient to explain the continued rise in land values. In fact when a second Labour Government was returned, albeit briefly, in 1950 many large landowners saw it as the death knell of private landownership. The Labour Government of 1945, which had sung 'The Red Flag' in the Chamber of the House and crowed 'We are the masters now', had a strong left-wing lobby dedicated to a policy of nationalization. Already one of the traditional props had been knocked from under the great landowners with the nationalization of the coalmines, and the 'privileges' of private landownership were one of the most emotive issues with the extreme left. It might well have been felt that the land boom had reached its apotheosis. It would have been a bold man who could have forecast with any confidence that the boom would continue as it did, although there were quite a few sagacious enough to read the straws in the wind and advocate a policy of agricultural expansion.

Whilst socialist ideology might have seemed to be inimical to the interests of landowners, their economic policy was not a harsh one. Although Tom Williams, the Minister of Agriculture, came under bitter attack by his own left wing for the 'feather-bedding' of farmers and other aspects of landownership such as forestry, which will be discussed later, much was done to ensure that the traditional postwar agricultural depression should not be repeated. Food prices were guaranteed, the development of marginal farmland heavily subsidized, and investment in capital equipment and buildings could be set against tax, thus enabling surplus income to be converted over a ten-year period into real wealth. Agricultural land enjoyed a 45 per cent relief on estate duty so that it became axiomatic that the safest hedge against inflation was in real estate. To add to this rosy picture, that other great standby of the large landowner (apart from financially advantageous marriages) – the ownership of urban property – was on the verge of an unprecedented boom.

5
The Urban Estates

It was pointed out earlier that few of the great landowners have been able to hang on to their territorial holdings without the accident of the discovery of mineral wealth or the development of their urban lands – often mere country villages which, with the coming of the Industrial Revolution, mushroomed almost overnight into large population centres. Obviously London, which in the space of scarcely a century exploded into being the largest and most important city in the world, was to rocket more families into the realms of the stratospherically rich than any other. Of all these, the Grosvenor family stand head and shoulders above the rest. Perhaps also they may be accounted one of the luckiest. As their development sets a pattern for many other – if less spectacular – fortunes it may be of interest to examine their history in some detail.

The Grosvenor family, one of the oldest in the kingdom, traces its ancestry back to Hugh Lupus, nephew of William the Conqueror and also his chief huntsman – a role which gave the family its name, Le Gros Veneur. The first Grosvenor property was a grant of land near Chester, and they have tenaciously held land in the area ever since. In 1450 Sir Thomas Grosvenor's second son married Joan of Eton, only child of John de Eton of Eaton, which has remained the family seat down to the present day. It would be hard to find a more typical example of the English aristocracy than the Grosvenor family. Love of country sports, involvement in local – and from time to time national – affairs and, above all, ability to keep the family ship afloat from generation to generation, characteristics of English families of long lineage, are all manifest. It was not until the mid-seventeenth century that events conspired to elevate their estate from comfortable prosperity to being the richest in the kingdom.

It is romantically believed that the acquisition of their London estates came about through one of the family falling in love with a milkmaid, whose father's farm consisted of the Manor of Ebury. The story goes that the careful farmer so mistrusted his daughter's suitor on account of his propensity for gambling that he created for her a trust of his lands which has survived to the present day. It is a charming story with little basis in truth. It is true that Sir Thomas Grosvenor did marry a Miss Mary Davies who was heiress to the Manor of Ebury, but she was never a milkmaid, her father was never a dairy farmer, and he did not create a trust. The real facts are very different and much more remarkable.

The story starts with Hugh Awdeley, who was born in 1577 and died at the age of eighty-five in 1662. Reports about him differ. Some claim that he was a usurer of the worst type, extracting every penny that he could from his victims. Others say that he was a fair-minded, upright man with a remarkable flair for business and particularly for property dealing. Whichever version is true does not now very much matter. The important fact was that he managed to accumulate an estate which, by the standards of the day, was vast. It was worth well in excess of half a million pounds and consisted of property spread all over England.

Hugh Awdeley outlived most of his close relatives, and was left in something of a dilemma about how to dispose of his wealth. Towards the end of his life his chief preoccupation was with making and remaking his will. The last version, made a few months before his death, bequeathed most of his best land to remote connections and friends. His nephew Alexander Davies, who had assisted his uncle in the management of his affairs, might have expected to be better rewarded than he was. Instead of rich farmland in Cambridgeshire or Bedfordshire he inherited what were to become the Manors of Ebury, Belgravia and Pimlico, but which at that time were undrained marshland on the outskirts of the city of London.

Alexander Davies was, however, a man of some vision. He set about developing his new property with great enthusiasm. He initiated an ambitious scheme to build a row of fine houses along Millbank, but died of the plague in his early thirties before they were finished. He left behind him a young widow, an only daughter, Mary Davies, and a pile of unpaid bills. The widow was not long in marrying again, and with her new husband John Tregonwell, she set about mending the broken financial fences. The operation was so successful that by the time her daughter reached the age of eight she was accustomed to drive out in her own coach, and was already being spoken of as a considerable heiress. The ambitious Mrs Tregonwell did not lose much time in finding a suitable match for her. Before the child was nine she was sold for £5,000 as the prospective wife of the ten-year-old Hon. Charles Berkeley, the son of Lord Berkeley of Berkeley House (Berkeley House occupied the site where Devonshire House now stands). The marriage contract also called for the settlement of £3,000 in land. When Lord Berkeley found himself financially unable to meet this additional commitment the bargain was called off, and it was not until she was thirteen that Mary Davies became affianced to Sir Thomas Grosvenor, whose town house stood near the Tregonwells' on Millbank. At first sight the marriage could not have seemed a particularly brilliant one. Sir Thomas had high social position and about £5,000 a year from his Cheshire estates and leadmines. Mary Davies had only a few acres of farmland, some building development in embryo and little social status.

It is, therefore, all the more pleasing to record that the marriage proved an extremely happy one. Sir Thomas remained devoted to his wife and she to him until he died in 1700, in spite of the fact that their last years together were clouded by her increasing mental instability. The happiness of their marriage had even survived Mary's conversion to Roman Catholicism at a time when anti-Catholic feeling was running high. It was a combination of her fiercely held religious beliefs and her unsound mental state which led to the extraordinary melodrama in which she became involved the year following her husband's death.

For some time she had been falling more and more under the influence of a Jesuit priest called Father Lodowick Fenwick, and it was he who suggested that she should make a pilgrimage to Rome on which he would accompany her as her spiritual adviser. It was on the return journey across France that Father Fenwick started to show himself in his true colours. One by one Lady Grosvenor's own servants were dismissed from her employ and sent back to England until she was entirely surrounded by people appointed by Fenwick. Worse, she had frequently recurring and inexplicable bilious attacks, when doctors would be called in at the instigation of Fenwick and severe bleeding prescribed as the sovereign remedy.

By the time the party reached Paris, where they put up at an hotel, the weakened and half-demented woman was virtually a prisoner. Hotel servants were later to depose that they were given orders that Lady Grosvenor was on no account to be allowed to leave her room, and that only three or four visitors named by Father Fenwick were allowed to visit her. Of these one was the priest's own brother, Edward Fenwick, whom Lady Grosvenor already knew and who had come from London to meet them. Later, too, there were servants who gave evidence of hysterical scenes when Lady Grosvenor threw dishes of food at the priest, refused to eat, and complained that she was being poisoned. Two servants said that they saw food being prepared with heavy doses of laudanum, and, if the lady could be persuaded to eat, that she was very quiet afterwards and often did not appear properly conscious of her surroundings. It is surprising in the circumstances that Lady Grosvenor returned to London accompanied by neither of the Fenwick brothers, but she was not to be left in peace for long.

Within a week of her return Edward Fenwick was also in London, declaring that he had been married to Lady Grosvenor in Paris and demanding his conjugal rights, the principal right being that he should receive the rental from her estates. His supposed wife hotly denied that she had ever entered into a marriage contract, and fled to Eaton at the insistence of her advisers, who feared that Fenwick might take her a prisoner and hold her by force.

The legal proceedings which followed became one of the *causes célèbres* of the century. Fenwick opened his offensive by warning the Grosvenor tenants that they were to pay their rents only to him, as the legal husband of Lady Grosvenor, or face eviction. The tenants in a body sought the protection of the court. Proceedings were started in France against Fenwick on the ground of abduction, which was punishable by death, but war with the French intervened and he escaped with his life. Back in England he petitioned to have his marriage legally recognized. Lady Grosvenor was lucky to find a champion of her cause in the person of her guardian, Charles Cholmondeley. As her bouts of insanity increased in frequency, he fought every inch of the way against the wily Fenwick; in 1701 her solicitors wrote: 'We are pressed on all sides very warmly in the Ecclesiastical Court, Chancery and Common Law.'

In the midst of these very serious processes, by which the Grosvenors might have lost all their London estates, a figure of pure comedy put in an appearance in the person of a Colonel Colepeper, who claimed that the Fenwick marriage could not be a valid one as he had himself previously contracted a marriage with Lady Mary. Whether his intervention was inspired by chivalry or hopes of gain are not apparent, and as he had no evidence to produce he was not taken very seriously. It was not until 19 February 1705 that, after one adverse decision upholding the marriage, the Court of Delegates pronounced that 'the said Court decrees that the said Dame Mary shall be absolved from all claim set forth by the said Edward [Fenwick] in his libel abovesaid, and that silence shall forever be imposed on him touching the same.' Luck was on the side of right.

Mary Grosvenor lived on under the care of Francis Cholmondeley, whose elder brother Charles had died before the dispute was settled. She outlived him also, and was commited to the care of Sir Richard Myddleton of Chirk Castle, where she died in 1730. Before she died, her three sons, each of whom in turn succeeded to the baronetcy, had begun the development of the Manor of Ebury, and Grosvenor Square and the surrounding streets had come into being. It was appropriate that one of the streets should have been named Audley after their original benefactor, and another Davies in memory of their luckless mother. Within the next hundred years the Davies inheritance was to become the most valuable land in the kingdom, and ultimately result in the descendants of Sir Thomas Grosvenor and Mary Davies being created Dukes of Westminster.

Like other old-established families the Grosvenors, in spite of their rapidly increasing wealth, retained all the characteristics of country landowners. They built a great town mansion, Grosvenor House which, until it was demolished in 1926, stood on the Park Lane site now

SIR FREDERICK RICHARD POWLETT MILBANK, 3rd Bt (1881–1964)   SIR MARK VANE MILBANK, 4th Bt (1907–1984)   SIR POWLETT MILBANK, 2nd Bt (1852–1918).

Five generations of a traditional landowning family: the Milbanks of Barningham Park, Yorkshire.

SIR ANTHONY FREDERICK MILBANK, 5th and present Bt (born 1939)   EDWARD MARK SOMERSET MILBANK (born 1973)   SIR MARK VANE MILBANK, 4th Bt.

SIR DAVID MONTGOMERY
Bt, JP, DL, Chairman of
the Forestry Commission.
He controls 2,917,000
acres. (*Forestry
Commission*)

LORD MANSFIELD, the first
Crown Estates
Commissioner, has
control of 268,000 acres.
(*By permission of the Crown
Estates*)

An aerial view of Castle Howard in Yorkshire. A jewel in the crown of the Howard family, branches of which own 27 castles including Arundel, the home of the Duke of Norfolk, hereditary Earl Marshal of England.

THE DUKE OF WESTMINSTER, owner of Mayfair and Belgravia, London's richest square mile of bricks and mortar. (*Times Newspapers Ltd.*)

The fabulously rich
Maktoum brothers
at the Ascot races.
They are heavy
investors in
bloodstock and
sporting land,
including one of
Yorkshire's finest
grouse moors.
(*Desmond O'Neill
Features*)

The Ritz Hotel in
Piccadilly. The site
of the town house of
the Walsingham
family, which was
sold to pay the
expense of having
Edward VII to
shoot pheasants on
their Norfolk estates.
(*Popperfoto*)

Chatsworth in Derbyshire, the seat of the Dukes of Devonshire and repository of one of the finest collections of art treasures in private hands in the world. (*Country Life*)

An unusual view of Sandringham in Norfolk. It was bought by the Royal Family as a sporting estate for the heir to the throne. (*Country Life*)

THE DUKE OF ROXBURGHE of Floors Castle, who owns 75,000 Scottish acres. (*BBC Hulton Picture Library*)

The New. Eaton Hall, the recently rebuilt family seat of the Dukes of Westminster. (*Country Life*)

The Old. Drum Castle, for centuries the property of the Irvine family and the oldest inhabited castle in Scotland, is now owned by the National Trust for Scotland. (*National Trust for Scotland*)

occupied by the Grosvenor House Hotel, and went there during the summer season to present their daughters at court and join in the fashion for lavish entertaining; but the centre of their existence was Eaton Hall. While wealth poured in in an ever-increasing flood from their urban developments, and Mayfair and Belgravia grew up as the most fashionable residential districts of London, they remained preoccupied with shooting and hunting over their country estates and in playing their part in local affairs. There was a time in their fortunes when it might have seemed logical to sell some of their mineral rights or agricultural holdings to finance the very much more profitable London developments, but it was not a policy which appealed to them. Instead, part of the London property was sold to provide the money to develop the remainder, and surplus funds were used to acquire more and more acres all over England and Scotland.

The acquisitive instincts of successive generations of Grosvenors were by no means limited to real estate. They were discriminating buyers of works of art, so that in the late nineteenth century the first Duke succeeded to one of the finest art collections in private hands in the country. He himself devoted much of his energies to establishing a stable of bloodstock which made Britain pre-eminent in the racing world – a position that she has never been able to claim since. The decision of the trustees to sell the horses on the death of the first Duke (his successor, the famous and colourful second Duke, Bendor, being on Kitchener's staff in South Africa at the time) was not only financially unnecessary but disastrous for British racing. It was as unnecessary as a later decision to sell some of the world's most famous pictures, including Gainsborough's *Blue Boy*. The bloodstock went to France and the finest pictures to America.

To set against these unfortunate lapses was the second Duke's decision to buy land and inaugurate a policy of urban development not only at home but overseas. In the years immediately after the Second World War estates were bought all over the country; and there were the spectacular development of Annacis Island on the west coast of Canada, and purchases in Australia and South Africa, amongst other overseas investments.

The second Duke was fortunate in having a quite exceptional Chief Agent to advise him in the person of George Ridley. It was Ridley who embarked on a policy of intensive development of both the London properties and the agricultural estates, where he was quick to take advantage of the subsidies on the development of farm buildings to increase productivity, which in turn would justify higher rentals. It was Ridley, too, who instituted the first major development of the London properties, selling much of the rather downmarket Pimlico area round

Victoria Station to finance the imaginative development of Eaton Square, which has led to Belgravia becoming the most prestigious residential area in London, usurping the prewar supremacy of Mayfair (also part of the Westminster estate), which has now bowed to the demand for high-quality office accommodation and hotels.

It is true that the postwar property boom which saw prices rocket into the stratosphere made many vast fortunes almost overnight for speculators and developers of various hues, but it is also true that, by and large, the great estates whose land holdings represent the richest acres in London have remained more or less intact despite onerous death duties and the constant threat of wealth tax as well as the very real factor of the soaring costs of maintenance. Only a very few of the great urban estates of the eighteenth century have lost their way – notably perhaps the Bedford estate, which had assiduously developed Bloomsbury as a fashionable residential area, only to lose much of it. Today the family only own a mere 30 acres scattered round the periphery of huge developments like London University, once the centre of their 'territory', whilst being denied the right to similar development of their Russell Square property by conservationist interests.

The shrewd Westminsters, by contrast, who still own all of 300 acres, have seen the reverse happen. Quite recently they were able to buy back the site of St George's Hospital, worth many millions of pounds, for a matter of £23,700 because their right to do so had been stipulated in a contract of sale drawn up in 1880. Many people felt that the Westminster trustees were being less than benign in insisting that the letter of the contract be upheld. On the other hand it is not often remembered that it was the Westminsters who led the way in remitting London rentals on their properties during the war years, when many of their properties were heavily blitzed, and that they also cut back on rentals for their agricultural properties during the depression of the 1930s, devoting part of their urban income to make this possible.

Although London today has spread its tentacles over some 500 square miles it is really only in the hard core of the metropolis, as it developed in the hundred and fifty or so years from 1700 to the mid-nineteenth century, that the pattern of urban ownership evolved. Interestingly there are only half a dozen families who have continued down the years to keep a firm grip on their family acquisitions or inheritances. A good example is the Howard de Walden estate, headed by the present ninth Lord Howard de Walden whose eminence in horse-racing circles is better known than his ownership of a hundred acres of London immediately north of Oxford Street. The estate includes such high-rental, rigorously controlled streets as Harley and

Wimpole where the medical profession pay stupendously to affix their brass plates on the exterior of Lord de Walden's bricks and mortar. Like the Bedfords' Bloomsbury estate, the de Walden acres came into the possession of the family by a happy series of political and matrimonial accidents. William of Orange, whose efforts to show his gratitude to his chief mentor, Hans Wilhelm Bentinck, resulted in the creation of the extensive Portland estates, did not omit to give the first Duke of Portland, in addition to great acreages of agricultural land, a cherry on top of the handsome cake in the form of some potentially even more advantageous gifts of land in fast-developing London. A daughter of the fourth Duke of Portland married the sixth Lord Howard de Walden in the mid-nineteenth century and brought with her an amalgamation of part Portland land and part Harley, Dukes of Oxford. Thus two more of the privileged 'inner six' became established – the remaining Portland land, some 55 rich acres, squeezed in between that of the de Waldens and that of the Church Commissioners.

The remaining three of the 'inner six' are the Church Commissioners and the Crown Commissioners, who will be discussed in Chapters 7 and 8, and the estate of the Cadogan family, which embraces much of Chelsea. The Cadogan estates are probably the most remarkable of the lot. Nobody could accuse the Cadogan family of being ungenerous: over-generous perhaps or even improvident, but the fact remains that the present Earl inherited an almost bankrupt estate in the early 1930s despite owning what was to become one of the most fashionable districts of London. Much of the prewar charm of Chelsea was its village-like quality, with many streets and even squares primarily developed as workmen's cottages, but they did not pay high rents. The estate, comprising 90 acres, was originally the property of Sir Hans Sloane, the founder of the British Museum, who bought it in 1745 and was responsible for much of the better development, as Hans Crescent, Street, and so on testify, and of course Sloane Street and Sloane Square, in the centre of which his statue bears witness to his vigorous influence. The whole partly developed estate came into the hands of the Cadogan family on the marriage of Hans Sloane's daughter to Lord Cadogan. The Cadogans were not particularly businesslike, and were given to acts of great generosity like the donation of some prime acres between Royal Hospital Road and the Embankment to the Royal Physical Society in perpetuity for the sum of £1 per annum. The Chelsea Physic Garden has remained established behind its high walls to this day, a monument to scientific learning and the generosity of the Cadogans. Today with a more streamlined management policy and a bull property market, the numerous two-up and two-down workmen's cottages fetch astronomical prices in the property market, and the

present Earl of Cadogan's heir, Viscount Chelsea, can assume his place
as one of the richest men in the country.

There were, of course, and still are a large number of families who
have quite substantial if less spectacular holdings. Bebbington, who
mapped some of these often quite difficult-to-trace family holdings
from street names – a sure giveaway – identified thirty-five in the
restricted area from Regents Park to the Thames. Up to the end of the
Second World War there were few substantial sales of urban property,
if one excepts the quite considerable sales in the nineteenth century to
bodies like the newly formed railway companies. The acquisition of
sites for Baker Street and Marylebone Stations, for example, bit deeply
into the Duke of Portland's once very large holdings. The diminution of
the Portland estate was accelerated by the sale of a further 150 acres of
Marylebone as recently as 1951 for the derisively small sum, by modern
reckoning, of around £7 million.

The most marked development on the London property scene – and
indeed in almost every other major centre of population throughout the
country – has been the activities of the development companies. In the
really boom years of the 'fifties and 'sixties the battle for new areas to
develop was ferocious. It was a matter of cobbling together blocks of
leaseholds and then, at the shadier end of the scale, of getting the
leaseholders to surrender their leases.

It was unusual – so tenaciously did existing owners hold on to their
properties – for the City Corporation at one blow to acquire the 110
acres which surround St Paul's, on which their spectacular if controversial Barbican development has taken place. More typical was the
hectic scrabble for land in the Buckingham Gate and Victoria Street
area. Almost all the largest property companies fought to get a foot in
the door. Many succeeded, with the result that one of the most
characterful areas of London, in the shadow of Westminster Abbey and
cheek by jowl with the Houses of Parliament, has been transformed into
a concrete jungle of high-rise office blocks with no attempt at aesthetic
co-ordination.

The utilitarian, profit-motivated architectural standards of the big
developers are worlds apart from the standards maintained by the large
nineteenth-century estates. The high standard of design and high
quality of materials set by builders like Thomas Cubitt, who was
responsible for much of the Grosvenors' Belgravia or Nash's elegant
Regents Park development for the Crown (although it must be
admitted that Nash's choice of materials was often somewhat
dubious!), will ensure that these buildings will still be standing
accusingly when many of the great modern slabs have outlived their
limited lifespan.

Another example of the reshuffling of the cards in this real-life Monopoly is the part played by the large institutional investors. It comes as something of a surprise to discover, for example, that British Petroleum's pension fund is backed by some £635 million of freehold bricks and mortar, including the whole of Berkeley Square; or that the amount of Prudential pension funds invested in real estate in London alone comes to over £1 billion.

By far the largest of the London landlords, however, are the various public authorities, of which the Port of London Authority is the biggest. There are hundreds of acres of disused railway land and land no longer needed by the Gas Boards. The now defunct Greater London Council had a large amount of land acquired originally for motorway construction but which, for one reason or another, is no longer needed for that purpose.* The inertia and lack of imagination shown by the various bodies concerned in disposing of their unwanted land for development show no signs of being resolved.

Although London is by far the most complex example of the importance to the great landowners of their urban possessions, it is not, as has already been remarked, in any way unique. Exactly why or how it came about that the Duke of Devonshire should have extensive property in Eastbourne, whilst the Dukes of Norfolk, in addition to their London holdings, should possess a large part of Sheffield, the Calthorpes south Birmingham or the Colman family most of Norwich, to mention only a few urban fortunes, would make a fascinating survey but one that is outside the scope of this work.

What does emerge is that, by and large, the record of the big urban landowners has been historically a good one – or, perhaps more realistically, it is only the good ones who have survived. It is only by the exercise of strict management rules and selectivity in the granting of leaseholds and licences that they have managed to keep their ships afloat. What is likely to prove increasingly outside their control is the manner in which the provisions of the Leasehold Reform Act come to be enforced. The Act provides for the right of leaseholders, under certain conditions, to purchase the freehold of their properties. It was originally passed to provide security of tenure for tenants in the lower income bracket, but it still applies to all tenants having properties with a rateable value of up to £1,500 in London and £750 elsewhere. Although applications are resolutely resisted, and particularly by London's 'big six', what the long-term effect of the Act will be is hard to forecast.

* The awkwardly named London Residuary Body, set up in 1985, was given five years to dispose of all the considerable GLC land holdings, a process which is continuing satisfactorily if not entirely without acrimony.

6

The Landed Classes Today

Within the social framework of Britain the Dukes have always occupied a special position. In theory they are the richest and the most territorially powerful of the aristocracy. They are traditionally addressed by the monarch as 'right trusty and entirely beloved cousins', and, by and large, live lives which are more remote from everyday affairs than those of the average run of aristocrats.

Of the twenty-six non-royal Dukes who survive today, most are of comparatively modern creation. Only two, Norfolk and Somerset, date from before the sixteenth century. Four Dukedoms, all of which survive, were created for the bastard sons of Charles II – Buccleuch by Lucy Walter, Grafton by Barbara Villiers, Richmond by Louise de Kérouaille and St Albans by Nell Gwynn. No fewer than eleven were created in the eighteenth century, of which only one, Marlborough, was for merit. All the rest were given to men promoted because they were powerful landowners. By contrast, there were only four promotions in the nineteenth century, of which the Duke of Wellington's was for merit. The last creation was in 1889, when the Earl of Fife was made a Duke following his marriage to Princess Louise, daughter of the Prince of Wales.

It now seems unlikely that any more Dukedoms will be created. The last to be offered one was Sir Winston Churchill, who refused it. To this extent Dukes may be said to be a dying breed. Much the same might be said of Marquises, none of whom has been created since 1931, when Lord Willingdon was made one on his retirement from the Viceroyalty of India.

The ranks of Dukes have been further depleted by the decision of three of them to make their homes abroad. Montrose and Newcastle have taken up residence in Zimbabwe, and Manchester has large estates in Kenya. Only one has fallen by the wayside financially in this century. The Duke of Leinster, whose family once owned 68,000 acres in Ireland, is now landless. His father was reduced to near penury in his lifetime through an unhappy series of financial accidents. The rest are probably as rich today as they have ever been and many a great deal richer, although as the table opposite shows, in most cases the number of acres that they own has been considerably diminished in the last hundred years. Indeed only Westminster and Roxburghe show any marked increase. They have also perpetuated the tendency amongst ducal families to intermarry, the most recent example being when the present Duke of Westminster's sister married the Duke of Roxburghe.

*Ducal Landholdings in the United Kingdom:**

	Acres in 1877	Acres in 1987
Norfolk	44,500	15,000
Somerset	25,500	7,000
Hamilton and Brandon	157,500	13,000
Buccleuch and Queensbury	459,000	252,000
Grafton	29,500	10,500
Richmond and Gordon	286,500	12,000
Beaufort	51,000	52,000
St Albans**	9,000	—
Devonshire	199,000	72,000
Bedford	87,500	21,000
Argyll	175,000	81,000
Marlborough	23,500	11,500
Atholl	194,500	120,000
Rutland	70,000	18.000
Roxburghe	60,500	75,000
Portland	162,000	64,500
Northumberland	186,397	80,000
Wellington	19,500	10,000
Sutherland	1,358,500	20,000
Abercorn†	65,000	—
Westminster	20,000	158,000
Fife††	259,000	—

* It is worth noting that, apart from the Westminster estates, these figures have not changed substantially in the last twenty-five years.
** The present Duke inherited no estate when he succeeded in 1964.
† The Abercorn estates are in Ireland, acreage not known.
†† The present Duke owns no land. On the death of the last Duke in 1959 the estates became separated from the title and were inherited by the present Duke's cousin, Captain Alexander Ramsay.

The trend for the great estates to diminish in size, if not in terms of actual wealth, is probably true in all strata of landowners. It is also made more striking when it is considered that in the last century two out of the top four landowners have dropped out of the league. The Marquis of Breadalbane's Scottish estates once totalled 438,000 acres, but the present Marquis does not own a single acre: they were largely lost over the gaming tables in the South of France; the Duke of Fife lost his estates through an accident of inheritance.

At the same time some of the largest landowners were not Dukes, notably the Earls of Derby who once owned a broad swathe of the Midlands including most of the land on which Liverpool was built. They also owned the whole of the Isle of Man, which carried with it a kingship. The present Earl's father, known affectionately as 'The King of Lancashire', died in 1948 and the estate came, like many others, under severe pressure from death duties, and the once vast properties started to diminish. None, however, can match the spectacular decline of the Dukedom of Sutherland, which was once the largest landowning family in the country, cobbled together, as we have already seen, through a succession of fortuitous marriages.

Although the fourth Duke, who died in 1963, managed to live in considerable state with a private railway to his Scottish seat, Dunrobin Castle, a steam yacht of great magnificence and a large estate, Sutton Place, outside Guildford, in addition to his almost limitless Scottish lands, it was very much a case of *après moi, le déluge*. In his lifetime he sold most of his Scottish lands to his relative and neighbour, the Duke of Westminster. (He, on his death, left Sutherland's estates to his widow, Anne, to enjoy for her lifetime, so presumably they will one day revert to the Westminster estate.) One by one the jewels of his crown were dismantled. The yacht went. His private railway and harbour closed. Sutton Place was bought by an American oilman, the late Mr Paul Getty, and finally even the titles became divided, for the fourth Duke left no male heir. Under Scottish law, which allows hereditary title to pass through the female line, his only daughter Lady Elizabeth Leveson-Gower, inherited the titles of Countess of Sutherland and Lady Strathnaver with Dunrobin Castle and 150,000 acres; whilst a distant kinsman, Lord Ellesmere, with a small estate of his own in the Borders, became the sixth Duke.

The reason for the decline of the Dukes of Sutherland's landed fortunes was partially, but only partially, due to the fact that their Highland estates comprised some of the poorest land in the country. The main factor, however, was that they had neither mineral nor urban wealth to support them in times of agricultural depression. It is all the more surprising, therefore, to find amongst landowning families today not a few examples of estates which have remained in the same family through thick and thin, with only their agricultural rentals to support them. A good example is the Yorkshire family of Milbanke.

The first baronetcy was created in the person of Sir Mark Milbanke in 1661, the son of a Mark Milbanke who inherited and added to what must have been a very considerable fortune made in trade in the emerging industrial area of Tyneside. He was a prominent – and therefore very rich – member of the Company of Merchant Venturers, incorporated by charter in 1547, which controlled most aspects of the economic and municipal life of Newcastle-upon-Tyne. It would appear that it was this Milbanke who first took the decision to acquire the considerable Milbanke estates in Durham and North Yorkshire and thus founded a landowning rather than an industrial dynasty for his successors.

The family lost and then regained the baronetcy – losing the 'e' from Milbanke in the process – and devoted themselves assiduously to looking after their estates with unusual consistency as each generation succeeded the previous one. Certainly there appear to have been some narrow squeaks in the family history. One, William Harry Vane Milbank, a nineteenth-century heir to the estates, chose to lead a buccaneering life on the Continent that matched, in the unlikeliness of the succession of 'episodes' in which he was involved, anything to which a modern James Bond could lay claim. He fought a series of duels, was banished at one time to the convict prisons of Siberia, and between times held open house in his luxurious residence in Paris, returning to the family seat at Barningham only briefly during the shooting season. In fact he never succeeded as he pre-deceased his father, perhaps fortunately. Surprisingly, he died only eight years before the turn of this century – of natural causes.

On the other side of the coin the Milbank family have had an occasional fortunate boost to their determined survival. Also about the turn of the century, the immensely wealthy Duke of Cleveland died. Having no direct heir, it is said that he had a will drawn up disposing of his various estates but leaving blanks to be filled in with the names of the ultimate beneficiaries. He signed it virtually on his deathbed, and under the circumstances it is not surprising that it was hotly disputed by disappointed expectant beneficiaries. It was, however, eventually proved, and William Harry's younger brother, Powlett Milbank, was agreeably surprised to find that he had inherited £400,000. In her meticulously kept diary Powlett Milbank's wife, who was a remote connection of the Duke, records laconically: 'Attended the Duke of Cleveland's funeral. Surprised to learn that we have inherited £400,000.' She did not allow herself the luxury of exclamation marks!

Equally, in the minutes recorded every month by the committee of Barningham library, which had been donated to the village by Sir Frederick Milbank and whose deliberations he regularly attended in the role of chairman, there is an entry which records the weighty decision to add the *Northern Echo* to the newspaper subscription list. This is followed by a motion congratulating Mr Powlett on his inheritance and expressing the hope that he would 'use it wisely'. Perhaps nothing demonstrates more clearly how families like the Milbanks have preserved their agricultural estates so successfully generation after generation. They have not sought to adventure into the extravagances of high living, so often the downfall of the young bloods of Regency and Edwardian times, but have identified with their tenantry, seeking by mutual support to steer the ship safely through good times and bad. There was not a local committee on which they did not serve nor a local government role they did not undertake.

As with almost all the big landowners, the present century has seen a shrinking in the size of the Milbank lands. In the agricultural depression of the 'thirties there were many who, in much the same position as the Milbanks, would have happily disposed of their lands had they been able to find a willing buyer. Indeed, when the present Sir Anthony Milbank inherited the Barningham estates from his father in the late 1960s there had already been grave family discussions about whether they could continue to survive much longer. It was a time when many of the old landowning families, fearful of the future, made the fateful decision to sell up. Today, with much of the land taken in hand and many new enterprises afoot to meet the challenges of modern estate ownership, the Milbank lands have weathered yet another phase in their long history.

The pattern of the changing face of landownership from the vast and generally underdeveloped estates of the landowners of previous centuries, and indeed, in some cases right up to the postwar era, is perhaps most simply demonstrated by looking at Scotland, where historically the estates have been both larger and less developed than in England. A survey carried out in the mid-nineteenth century shows that of Scotland's estimated 19 million acres no less than 7½ million, over a third of the total land area, were in the hands of thirty-five individuals. Today almost half these landowners have disappeared from the scene for one reason or another (including the Dukes of Sutherland and the Marquises of Breadalbane, who between them held a disproportionate 2 million acres). Of the survivors only the Duke of Buccleuch, with an estimated 252,000 acres now the largest private landowner in the country, still retains a really substantial land holding by the standards of the last century.

There now remain in private hands approximately 16,500,000 acres. Of these almost half consist of estates of under 1,000 acres – in other words, really large farms or multiple farms, most of which are owner-occupied. In 1970 it was estimated that the top hundred landowners in Scotland owned 5 million acres. Today the total would be substantially less. At the same time the amount of state-owned land, as represented largely by the Forestry Commission, which owns some 3 million acres, is increasing rapidly. Although the Forestry Commission's acreage is by far the largest, other bodies have substantial holdings, with the Department of Agriculture getting on for a million acres and British Rail, the National Coal Board and the Ministry of Defence all coming into the category of large to very large landowners.

There is a further complication in analyzing how land ownership is shifting in the growing number of institutional investors. It was a trend which started in the early 1970s and was a considerable factor in accelerating the steep rise in the value of land. Looking at the influence of institutional investors in the land market in Great Britain, it has been estimated that today thirty times more money is available through the various financial investment brokers than is required to buy every single acre of prime agricultural land which comes on to the market.

Richard Norton-Taylor, in his 1982 survey entitled *Whose Land Is It Anyway?* (Twinstone Press), claims that between 1971 and 1978 the City interest in farmland increased from a mere 50,000 acres to at least 500,000 acres. This is probably a considerable underestimate. Land transactions, particularly where investing bodies like insurance companies and pension funds are involved, are generally shrouded in secrecy to an extent that is sometimes impenetrable. What is certain is that only a very small proportion of Britain's farmland ever comes on to the open market, and of the land which does change hands probably well over half is bought by institutions, including such unlikely buyers in the public mind as trade unions. Even more improbable was the considerable investment made by bodies like British Rail in works of art and antiques. It is reckoned that whilst the great country houses like Mentmore (Rothschild), Hever Castle (Astor), Elvedon (Guinness) and even Chatsworth (Devonshire) are one after another putting their incomparable collections of pictures, furniture and other treasures on the market, to fetch prices that make even Christie's and Sotheby's gasp, quiet, shrewd men representing the interests of tens of thousands of ordinary working citizens are buying in the certainty that they have the soundest of long-term investments.

Richard Norton-Taylor asserts that from a modest toe-in-the-water beginning in land investment by insurance companies and pension funds in the early 1960s, by the 1980s there were very few indeed who were not heavily committed. That in the 'sixties there were only a few who were confidently forecasting a sharp rise in the price of land from around £100 an acre to £300 an acre is a tribute to the sagacity of the few. It is safe to say that none could anticipate that by the end of the 1980s the price would be £2,000 an acre and in many cases considerably more.

'We all know it now,' *The Times* has already been quoted as saying in 1919, 'England is changing hands.' Sixty-five years later it is truer than ever and the speed with which it is changing hands is not slowing down; it is accelerating. If the institutions which represent the greater part of the general public continue on their present policy and their present rate of acquisition of large agricultural holdings, they will control half of Britain's total food production by the turn of the century as well as most of the country's timber resources. It goes a long way towards explaining why, despite the recurrent lobbying by left-wing politicians for the nationalization of land, successive Governments, and perhaps particularly socialist administrations, continue to introduce progressive legislation to protect the interests of the landowners, for the interests of the landowners are becoming more and more identified with the interests of the people. The great landowning classes of the eighteenth and nineteenth centuries, with all their faults and virtues, are today almost as extinct as the dodo.

7

The Royal Estates

The monarchy has always been a landowner to a greater or lesser degree. In a way, land might be described as the currency of kingship. It was the means of rewarding loyal subjects, and, by its confiscation, a way of punishing the disloyal. It provided the basis for financing royal wars, and for many centuries dictated the extent of the sovereign's dependence on Parliament. A monarch who had rich land revenues could afford to be much more autonomous than one who had to go cap in hand to Parliament for financial support.

Although the Saxon kings had owned considerable areas of land, the first really great landowner was William I. By the time his conquest of England was complete, his personal estate was estimated as a fifth of the whole kingdom. His successors pursued a policy of alienation – the granting of land to favoured subjects as rewards or in expectation of their support. These alienations generally exceeded in extent the amount of new lands acquired by the confiscation of malefactors' estates. By the reign of Henry VII, however, the royal estates were again vast, probably even larger than those held by William the Conqueror. They again declined during the reign of Henry VIII, who was saddled with expensive wars. The seizure of monastic lands may have had a political excuse, but it was also economically expedient: the appropriation of over eight hundred land-rich monasteries made him, fleetingly, the greatest landowner in the history of these islands; but, by the time of his death they had largely been sold to raise ready cash.

Charles I pledged his lands to the City of London for £320,000, to finance the Civil War: by the time of the Restoration, the extent of the royal lands was again seriously depleted. William III celebrated his success in establishing a revolutionary Government by making lavish gifts of land to his Dutch supporters – notably Bentinck, Earl (later Duke) of Portland, and Keppel, Earl of Albemarle. So prodigal was William that, when he proposed to add a handsome slice of Denbigh to the already large Portland estates, Parliament protested vigorously and he was forced to withdraw the gift. Although he worked hard at the task of divesting himself of his lands, the Crown Estates have one reason today to be grateful to him. It was William who bought Nottingham House from the Earl of Nottingham. The pleasure grounds are now Kensington Gardens, and what were once the servants' quarters and kitchen gardens of old Nottingham House now yield a handsome income to the Crown, in the form of ground rents from Kensington Palace Gardens and Palace Green.

The nadir of the royal fortunes came with the reign of Queen Anne: it has been estimated that her landed wealth brought in no more than £6,000 a year. Matters were so serious that, by an Act of Parliament in 1702, the sovereign's power to dispose of land was severely limited. This marked the beginning of the realization that the royal lands had an important part to play in providing what is now generally known as the Civil List. The Civil List dates, in fact, from 1698, when Parliament granted William of Orange a fixed annuity to support his household. This annuity was made up from such hereditary revenues as customs and excise duties and, of course, the profits on landed estate.

It was not until George III came to the throne in 1760 that the granting of the Civil List assumed the form which has been followed to the present day. It is an historic date in the history of the Crown lands, for it marked a complete change in attitude. For the first time a clear line of distinction was drawn between what the monarch owned in his private right as an individual and what he owned 'in right of the Crown'. In return for a guaranteed income, George III surrendered the surplus revenues from all the Crown lands for his lifetime. If the Crown lands prospered he did not benefit financially, but on the other hand he was buffered against a decrease in their value. This surrendering the profits from the Crown lands in return for a fixed annuity still remains a voluntary act by each sovereign at the time of his or her accession. The sovereign has in fact the right to refuse the Civil List, but with the passing of time it has become so much a convention that it would be a very hard practice to discontinue.

From the time of George III the fortunes of the Crown lands have flourished mightily, thanks very largely to a decision to develop those in London which are now known as Regents Park, Regent Street and Waterloo Place. For the purpose £600,000 was borrowed in 1820, and Nash was appointed to lay out the new development area. This resulted not only in a rich architectural inheritance but also in a golden investment for the Crown.

Because of the way in which the Crown Estates have grown up and become gradually separated from the private land holdings of the sovereign, a great deal of confusion is bound to exist in the public mind as to where one set of interests ends and the other begins. It is interesting, therefore, to examine exactly what lands and rights are surrendered to the state in return for the grant of the Civil List.

The agricultural land in England vested in the Crown Estates is spread over twenty-seven counties and amounts to a total of 176,400 acres. It varies in origin from ancient manors which have survived the vicissitudes of centuries, such as Muchland at Aldingham in Lancashire, to new additions like Sunk Island, reclaimed from the Humber estuary. The Scottish estates extend to a further 87,407 acres. Some of this land, for example in Caithness, derives from acquisitions at the time of the abolition of the episcopacy in 1689, but by far the greater bulk of the Scottish lands, almost 70,000 acres, was purchased from the Duke of Richmond and Gordon as recently as 1937. As most of the Richmond and Gordon estate consisted of particularly bleak moorland and hill, it is hard to understand what prompted this particular purchase. The Welsh estates are almost entirely made up of land acquired during the thirteenth and fourteenth centuries, and consist of a large number of manorial wastes subject to grazing and common rights. The Crown also owns the mineral rights under about 320,000 acres.

The urban estates are made up almost exclusively of some of the highest rental areas in London, although they also include part of Dover and much of Portland as well as the Royal Blackheath, Eltham Warren and Richmond Golf Clubs. In London, the main groups of residential property are at Cumberland Market, which lies near Regents Park, Millbank, and Victoria Park to the east, with outlying properties at Fulham, Lee Green, Blackheath and Eltham, in Victorian times one of London's most fashionable suburbs. Aesthetically the brightest jewels are the architecturally magnificent Nash terraces by Regents Park and the highly prestigious houses in Kensington Palace Gardens. In purely commercial terms, however, the Estate has nothing to match their office properties in St James's, Pall Mall, Piccadilly, Haymarket and Regent Street. Also included in the lands controlled by the Commissioners for the Crown Estates is the Windsor estate, although the Castle itself, as an official royal residence, is the responsibility of the Ministry of the Environment.

The attitude of the Commissioners towards their Windsor responsibility is a mixture of pride that it is there at all and unease at the fact that it costs them something in the order of £2 million a year to maintain its 2,000 acres of farmland and 7,500 acres of woodland, which require a staff of ninety foresters as well as sundry other specialist workmen. There is also the Great Park of 4,000 acres, most of which is open to the general public. A further considerable expenditure is involved in the maintenance of the Saville and Valley Gardens in the Great Park, which alone employ a staff of fifty gardeners. The whole business of running the Crown Estates occupies a headquarters staff of 130 and an outside staff of around 500, of whom 300 are employed at Windsor.

The Queen's possessions as administered by the Crown Commissioners are not confined to real estate. She owns, for example, the

seabed which surrounds her kingdom, and even the right, by international agreement, to all minerals on the Continental Shelf under the
North Sea. The right of the Crown to superficial minerals below the
mean high-water mark was the basis of a famous dispute in the middle
of the nineteenth century, when it was brought to the attention of the
Crown that the Earls of Lonsdale had for generations been making a
vast income from undersea coalmines at Whitehaven in Cumberland.
Rather belatedly, the Crown protested that its rights had been illegally
usurped and demanded that the mines be handed over. The third Earl
blandly replied that access to the mines could only be obtained by
trespass on his land, and if he could not work the mines nobody else
should. The Crown countered this by demanding that his lordship pay
£100,000 to settle the dispute. Lonsdale replied that he would consider a
sum of £5,000 on the grounds that the mines were already becoming
worked out. The argument went on in a desultory way for over thirty
years, until the fourth Earl agreed to pay the sum of £50,000. It proved a
good bargain. Far from becoming worked out, the undersea seams
became richer and richer until, by 1910, over 3,000 tons of first-quality
coal a day were pouring from the pithead conveyor belts.

With the reorganization and rationalization of the Lowther estates
after the war, coupled with the nationalization of the coalmines, the
whole of the once prosperous seaport of Whitehaven, which had become
almost exclusively a mining town, was sold off, but the Lowthers, in
their thousand years of history, have proved themselves nothing if not
resourceful and persistent. Thinking to find a flaw in the complicated
mesh of negotiations down the years, the trustees of the estate sued the
Crown as recently as 1980 for the restitution of certain rights. The case
went to the House of Lords and the trustees lost. Happily this *cause
célèbre* does not appear to have affected the warm relationship between
the present Earl and the royal family, who still turn out regularly for the
famous carriage driving trials now held annually in Lowther Park.

Apart from owning the seabed, the Queen also owns most of the land
round the coast of Britain between the high- and low-water marks; the
only exceptions are some stretches owned by one or other of the royal
duchies. Today this is proving a most valuable asset to the Crown
Commissioners. Reclaimed land, such as in the area of the Wash,
automatically becomes the property of the Crown, and the revenue
from the selling of marine sand and gravel is considerable. In fact the
demand is so great that many of the traditional areas are becoming
exhausted and surveys are at present being carried out to investigate
the possibility of dredging sand and gravel from new areas of the
seabed. In all, the income from the mineral and other rights on the
seabed amounts to more than £2 million a year.

There is only one main exception to the Queen's ownership of the foreshore, and it is a curious one. In the Orkney islands, a freeholder owns his land under udal law, one of the peculiarities of which is that his land is considered to extend to the lowest point of the ebb tide. It is a valuable concession, for many of the islanders feed their sheep on the seaweed, and the tangle washed up on the foreshore is in ever greater demand as the alginate industry expands. Udal law derives from the time when the Orkneys were owned by Norway. At the time of the marriage of Margaret of Norway to James IV of Scotland in 1468, her dowry was set so high that King Christian could not raise the money. Instead he pledged the Orkneys and Shetland, on the understanding that they would continue to be governed by Norse law, and that the pledge could be redeemed whenever the money could be raised. It has been suggested that Norway could still reclaim both groups of northern isles on payment of 60,000 florins (£45,000). Unlikely though this is, the Norse udal law has remained in force on the islands, as a surprised Admiralty found to their cost after the Second World War. Having built a pier on one of the islands for naval use during the war, they tried to claim rent for it when it reverted to civilian use only to discover that, under udal law, it was they who owed the landowner rent for having put it there in the first place!

Careful management since the days of Queen Anne has transformed the Crown Estate into one of the richest in the country. It now yields a net annual income of substantially over £30 million, which is paid over to the state and out of which the Civil List is paid to the Queen. The figure agreed when the Queen came to the throne in 1952 was £475,000 – an advance on the amount granted to George VI, who had £410,000. This annual payment is not subject to fluctuation with the rise and fall of the cost of living, so that today the Queen is very much worse off than she was at the time of her accession. Just the same, the size of the Civil List is a favourite subject of attack by extreme left-wing politicians. In fact the financial advantage to the state accruing from the Crown lands is a very substantial one.

Since the last war the administrative machinery of the Crown Estate has undergone a considerable overhaul to bring it up to date. This rethinking came about as a direct result of the famous case at Crichel Down in Dorset, which involved land compulsorily acquired by the Air Ministry in 1937. When, by 1953, it was no longer required, an arbitrary attempt was made to transfer it to the Commissioners for Crown Lands, and to ignore the rights of the successors to the original owner. The case which the family brought to establish their right made headline news, and has an embarrassment value for the Crown Commissioners to this day. As a result of an inquiry into the management of the Crown lands the Crown Estate Act of 1956 was introduced, setting up a new constitution. The old board of two ministers and a senior civil servant was swept away, and a new board of eight known as the Crown Estate Commissioners was set up. This board consists of a part-time First Commissioner, who is currently the Earl of Mansfield, as chairman, and a deputy chairman who is usually recruited from the Civil Service; the other Commissioners are either large landowners or experts with special skills in estate management, farming and accountancy.

The record of the Commissioners has been a good one. They have shown commendable determination to preserve what is architecturally worthwhile, such as the Nash terraces on the south side of Regents Park, and at the same time to be in step with modern trends and new building developments, which have included New Zealand House and the *Economist* building. At Windsor, where financial considerations might have dictated a different policy, the Commissioners have continued to improve rather than restrict the facilities offered to the public and, although their forestry operations were rather slow to get off the mark in the postwar period, they would now seem to be set on a more constructive course which is in marked contrast to the scanty attention paid for many years to this important aspect of estate management.

Apart from the lands which go to make up the Crown Estate, the Queen owns very large acreages as her personal property. Indeed, if the lands of the Duchy of Cornwall were to be included, she would be the largest private landowner in the country. The Duchy lands, however, are only held in trust by her until the male heir to the throne comes of age. They then provide a private income for him until he in turn inherits the throne. Their history is an interesting one.

In 1337 Edward III created his eldest son (later to be known as the Black Prince) Duke of Cornwall. At the same time, 'that he might be able to sustain the state and honour of the said Duke according to the nobility of his birth', he granted him lands in Devon and Cornwall. The Duchy so created has remained the perquisite of the male heir to the throne ever since. Since those early days, when its most valuable assets were its mineral rights, the estate has gone through many vicissitudes. It once included such outlying properties as Castle Riding and Knaresborough – long since sold in the interests of easier management – but it is still sufficiently diversified as to own flower farms in the Isles of Scilly, the Oval Cricket Ground in London and the head lease of Dartmoor Prison. In the land return of 1874, the extent of the Duchy lands is shown as 69,502 acres, but, as Bateman remarks, 'the lead mines were unrated and unentered. The chief value of the Duchy is in its Devon and Cornwall mines, of which the very best workings are on lead.' Today there are no mines still in operation, but the acreage has been considerably extended. It now amounts to just under 140,000 acres, although it must be remembered that over 80,000 of these are contained in Dartmoor, from which income is derived from a mere twenty-nine workable farms. The remaining 60,000 acres, however, are made up of 250 farms let on annual tenancies or leaseholds, with a further ninety flower farms on the Isles of Scilly.

The lands of the Duchy of Cornwall extend across six counties in the West Country, 4,000 acres on the Scilly Isles, 160 miles of foreshore and 11,000 acres of riverbed. The 45-acre Kennington estate on the south bank of the Thames includes the Oval Cricket Ground which is let at such a modest rental that the two-bedroom flat in Kennington rented by James Callaghan brings in almost as much income. The only land farmed 'in hand' by the Duchy management is the 125-acre Home Farm at Stoke Cousland in Cornwall, but according to figures published in 1983 total rentals from let land produced an income of £575,000 in that year – a figure which, at a conservative estimate, has now doubled.

Following a tradition started by his great-uncle, Edward VIII, in his bachelor days the present Prince of Wales paid half of the income (which is tax-free although he does pay rates) to the Treasury. However, after his marriage to Lady Diana Spencer in 1981 he reduced this to 25 per cent. He has also adopted a more aggressively commercial approach towards the management of his estates, dramatically increasing rents, in some cases by as much as 90 per cent although, in this connection, it should be pointed out that over the years many properties had been let at rates which were absurdly low. Quite apart from the lands which he holds by right of being heir to the throne, in 1981 the Queen bought Highgrove House for him with an estate of 347 acres, at a cost believed to be between £750,000 and £1 million.

Rather less colourful but no less important is the Duchy of Lancaster, which is also part of the Queen's estate. The Duchy was created by Henry III, again in favour of his heir, and it recently celebrated the completion of seven hundred years as a royal estate. It has its administrative offices in a modest building in Holborn, and is not to be confused with the office of the Chancellor of the Duchy of Lancaster, which is a political appointment and operates from Whitehall. The lands of the Duchy consist of some 52,000 acres spread over the counties of Yorkshire, Lancashire, Cheshire, Staffordshire and Northampton-shire. It comprises some of the best agricultural land in the country and provides a substantial income, estimated at approximately £500,000 a year.

Although the two Duchies make a very large contribution to the land wealth of the Queen, neither provide her with a private house or with the sporting facilities which normally go with a large estate, nor indeed with a personal income. To this extent they are almost as impersonal a possession as the Crown lands. By contrast, Queen Elizabeth I had no fewer than fourteen palaces dotted about the countryside, and Henry VIII before her had more than twenty. In those early days, most of the royal year was taken up with travelling with the court from house to house, to 'show the flag' and to impress the local populace with the reality of the monarchy. With the progressive diminution of the royal landed wealth it became impossible to maintain so many establishments, nor with improved communications was it necessary to do so. The houses were sold off one by one, and in time royal tours in various parts of the country took the place of annual visits.

It was Queen Victoria who first felt the need for more privacy for herself and her family than could be provided by the official residences of Buckingham Palace, Windsor Castle and the seldom visited Holyroodhouse outside Edinburgh. When she came to the throne, the only private residence possessed by the royal family was George IV's Brighton Pavilion, an edifice not at all to the taste of the new Queen. She sold it not long after her accession, and used the money to buy Osborne House on the Isle of Wight from Lady Blanchford in 1845 together with 1,000 acres of surrounding land to give her the privacy she so earnestly desired. The price paid was a modest £26,000, but soon afterwards, encouraged by the Prince Consort, the whole of Osborne was rebuilt and furnished at a cost of £200,000; even this figure was achieved only by dint of such economies as hiring a piano instead of purchasing one outright.

It was not long after the purchase of Osborne that the Queen and the Prince Consort travelled to Scotland to stay as guests of the Marquis of Breadalbane at his Perthshire seat, Taymouth Castle. The royal couple fell deeply in love with the remoteness of the Scottish hills and with all things Scottish. There followed a painstaking search for a suitable Scottish holiday home, which ended when the Queen bought Balmoral Castle, on the headwaters of the Dee in Aberdeenshire, from the Gordon family. There the same policy was followed as at Osborne. No sooner was the property secured than it was pulled down, and the turreted, granite edifice which we know today rose in its place. In her enthusiasm for her Scottish home Queen Victoria had the walls covered with stags' heads, and embellished it with specially designed tartan wallpaper and carpets. Even the linoleum in the servants' quarters was in a tartan pattern, and the candlesticks with which guests were lighted to bed were made in the shape of Highlanders in full dress.

The acquisition of Balmoral did not satisfy the Queen's territorial ambitions. For the growing Prince of Wales she bought the house and estate of nearby Birkhall, and when that house proved too small for him tried to buy Abergeldie Castle, which was also owned by the Gordon family. On this occasion the family could not be persuaded to sell but agreed to lease it – an arrangement which has continued to the present day.

It was Queen Victoria, or, more accurately, the Prince Consort, who was also responsible for the purchase of Sandringham – again for the benefit of the Prince of Wales. This purchase was a result of the Prince Consort's careful management of the royal finances, and an example of his long-sightedness. Realizing that the time would come when the Prince of Wales would require an English establishment of his own, he carefully husbanded the income from the Duchy of Cornwall, so that when the time came he was able to find the considerable sum of £220,000 which was required to buy Sandringham from the Hon. Charles Spencer Cowper, a stepson of Lord Palmerston, and provide a further £60,000 to alter it to the requirements of the heir to the throne. Sandringham was, perhaps, the most surprising of the royal purchases. Set in one of the bleakest parts of Norfolk, it was not in its original form an attractive house. In the end a further vast sum of money had to be spent on it before the Prince of Wales was satisfied, but it was to prove one of the favourite royal properties. Edward VII was never happier than when at Sandringham, and in later years George V was to say of it: 'Dear old Sandringham the place I love better than anywhere else in the world.' It was a sentiment which George VI would certainly have endorsed.

One member of the royal family who had little time for Sandringham was Edward VIII. He thought the amount of money spent on rearing pheasants was a waste, and was impatient of such experiments as the flax farming which had been introduced by his father, George V. When he succeeded, one of his first acts was to order drastic economies, and he seldom went there, preferring the comfort of Fort Belvedere. Today, Sandringham is a mixture of the traditional and the up-to-date. It is still a fine pheasant shoot, although the bags are not as heavy as they used to be. More money is spent on improving the farms and less on maintaining the game coverts. Prince Philip, with his love of the progressive, has introduced many new ideas. The once huge staff of gardeners has now been considerably reduced by the introduction of mechanization.

When Queen Victoria died, Osborne was never lived in again by the royal family. Instead, in 1902, the land on the Isle of Wight was made over to the Crown Estate and the house opened to the public, to form, as the old Queen had wished, a memorial to her beloved husband. Sandringham and Balmoral, however, have remained part of the private estate of the royal family, to be testated from one generation to the next. Thus when Edward VIII abdicated, both the estates were in his private possession and his brother was obliged to buy them from him.

Balmoral remains the Queen's favourite as well as her largest private estate. As recently as 1977 she added a further 7,500 acres of grouse moor which she bought from a neighbouring estate. Today the whole of the Balmoral estate probably exceeds 50,000 acres, but otherwise little has changed. Much of the tartan furnishings, now rather faded, remains from Queen Victoria's day, and the Queen takes just as great an interest in the estate and her tenants as did her great-great-grandmother. The two-month holiday break, when they follow the traditional sports of salmon fishing and grouse shooting, is much looked forward to by the royals, although a nine-hole golf course was created some years ago for the convenience of those guests who do not feel up to more vigorous pursuits. Since Prince Charles's marriage there has been much speculation in the popular press as to whether Princess Diana is enamoured of the royal traditions. That is, of course, just one of the penalties to be paid for the increasing intrusiveness of the media into the life of the royals and perhaps most resented at Balmoral, the traditionally very private royal retreat.

The Queen is generally considered to be amongst the richest women in the world. Her personal ownership of works of art (including a stamp collection worth over £1 million) must make her, at least on paper, an extraordinarily wealthy woman. As a private landowner, however, the 7,000 acres she owns at Sandringham and the 50,000-odd acres at Balmoral do not put her in the first flight of private landowners, even allowing for the depleted acreages of the really big estates. (It is often said that Queen Victoria invested in real estate in America, and that it forms part of the Queen's private fortune today. This seems, on the face of it, unlikely.)

Certainly in the eighteenth century the monarch could not be counted as being as wealthy as some of his subjects, and Buckingham Palace was just another town house with which many of the great landowners could vie in splendour. With the levelling-down process over the years, only the royal way of life has survived – a pinnacle in the middle of a plain, rather than the apex of a mountain. The great town houses have disappeared and the landowners no longer play a part in the constitutional life of the country. Buckingham Palace, with its 45 acres of private gardens, remains alone, marooned in a sea of bricks and mortar – or rather of concrete and glass.

In the speculation which breaks out almost annually in the media as to who are the world's richest people, the Queen is always included amongst the top fliers together with Arab sheiks and rather mysterious American names who count their fortunes in billions of dollars. Were Prince Charles, when he succeeds to the throne as King Charles III, to relinquish the Civil List, which now stands at £5.2 million a year, and retain all the profits from the royal estates, as will be his indisputable right, it would certainly put him very near the top of the league of the richest men in the world. He is known not to relish the role of holding out the beggar's bowl to the state for everything. In 1987 the Crown Commissioners broke with their secretive traditions to announce that the urban properties and the acreage of land owned by the Queen were valued at £1,277 million. The annual benefit that the state derives from the royal lands is therefore a very considerable one, despite the persistent howling on the political left that the royal family is a ridiculously expensive anachronism.

8

The Church

The Church of England is traditionally and actually amongst the largest landowners in the country. It is also very rich. That it should constantly be seen to be holding out the begging bowl claiming that it has insufficient funds to help the countless parish churches up and down the country, which would appear to be in constant need of reroofing, or indeed to pay its clergy a more generous stipend, has led to accusations of rapacity by the general public and, in certain aspects, to misunderstanding among its own servants.

This perhaps is not surprising, for it is only over the last couple of decades that the Church has not sought to conduct its affairs behind a cloak of secrecy, and only since the end of the last war that it has made serious and professional efforts to set its financial house in order. In the past the Church had no central treasury. Its money and lands belonged to individual parishes, some of which were very rich and some very poor, and to various cathedrals, dioceses and bishoprics. There were two main bodies concerned with trying to distribute the income of the Church as equitably as possible: Queen Anne's Bounty and the Ecclesiastical Commissioners.

Before the break with Rome, whenever a benefice fell vacant the new incumbent was required to remit the equivalent of one year's income to the Pope. After the dissolution of the monasteries, the monarch became the recipient of these monies. Queen Anne created her Bounty in the eighteenth century by handing these funds back to the Church. The Ecclesiastical Commissioners came into being in the nineteenth century by Act of Parliament.

One of the first tasks of the Ecclesiastical Commissioners was to try to iron out the anomalies created by the great individual wealth of the bishops' estates in particular, and the wealthier parishes in general. It had become common practice for individuals anticipating a happy life in the hereafter to leave land to the parish in which they had worshipped – this was known as the glebe – or to endow the church with a proportion of their land's produce, which was known as the tithe. In this way some parishes became entirely self-supporting, and bishoprics waxed fat from their inheritances. Some, inevitably, waxed fatter than others. The bishops of London, for example, found that modest gifts of land on the outskirts of the capital suddenly became immensely valuable as the need grew for land to house the rising population. A striking instance is the 200-acre farm on which Paddington was built.

This was to become one of the brightest jewels in the church's treasury, but it has also laid the Church open to more public criticism than the rest of its property put together, for reasons discussed later in this chapter.

The Church was supported almost entirely by the landowners in the days when the landowners were omnipotent. It relied on them for its material wellbeing, and the clergy vied for the landowners' favour in obtaining the best-endowed livings. The squire and his family occupied the front pew, and their household servants trooped in behind them in order of precedence to occupy the pews further back. When the service was over the whole congregation stood in respectful silence while the gentry filed down the aisle to their waiting carriages. In return for this patronage, it was expected that the clergy would inveigh against the sins of loose living and sloth, and point to the road to salvation which lay in diligently serving one's master.

The Church accepted its dependence on the landowners as being in the natural order of things. Indeed, it was unreasonable to expect them to do otherwise. Many of the clergy were themselves scions of the great landowning families, for the Church, like the Army, was viewed as a suitably gentlemanly occupation for a younger son. The parson who hunted four days a week and regularly had his bottle of port after dinner was regarded as a fine example to his parish, and was an object of envy to his brothers of the cloth who could not afford to follow his example.

Even if the Church had been of a mind to alter the *status quo* in the spacious days of the eighteenth century, it would have been quite unable to do so. Its increasing wealth was widely dispersed, so that its power to control its own corporate destiny was limited. A clergyman in charge of a rich living was independent of any means of coercion, and his way of life entirely a matter between himself and his patron. Neither his bishop nor his congregation could dictate to him the manner in which he should carry out his duties. The resulting image of the parson as part of the upper social structure, rather than as a refuge for the spiritually needy, was a long time in passing – indeed, may still exist in some country areas today.

The changes which took place in the Church in its attitude towards its own inheritance were forced upon it by sociological considerations rather than spiritual ones. By the beginning of the nineteenth century the whole social structure of the country had fundamentally altered. The new industrial parishes with their closely packed slums did not appeal to most of the established clergy, but they presented a challenge which the Church could not afford to ignore. New churches had to be built and sufficient clergy found with the necessary missionary zeal. The new churches were unendowed with either glebe land or tithes.

The livings carried with them no social cachet and meant exchanging a life of leisured independence for one of unremitting and unrewarding toil. As a result, Methodism flourished most vigorously where poverty was greatest and where the Church of England found itself without the men or the means to cope with the new conditions.

Queen Anne's Bounty did not have either the power or the wealth to deal with the needs of the situation – which amounted to no less than a need to overhaul the financial structure of the Church. But when the Ecclesiastical Commissioners came into being in 1836 they undertook the function of making 'additional provision for the cure of souls'.

The undertaking started slowly. Initially, the only monies which the Commissioners could lay their hands on were the ancient endowments of various cathedral dignitaries which had been suppressed, and the revenue from a number of outdated sinecures. The next step was to attack the financial power of the sees. At first the great estates of the bishops remained in their owners' control, but the revenue was channelled into a pool administered by the Commissioners; out of this, provision was made to ensure an income for newly created sees such as Manchester and Ripon, and an attempt was made to secure a more equitable distribution of Church wealth.

This was a slow process, since it was not for almost half a century that the Commissioners felt able to promote the next logical step. In 1860 an Act was passed enabling the Commissioners to acquire the estates themselves, in return for granting the bishops a fixed – and substantial – income, or re-endowing the see with sufficient land to provide such an income. The first alternative was an arrangement which seems to have met with the approval of the bishops, for in the thirteen instances where estates were re-endowed they were later handed back to the Commissioners to manage in return for the fixed income. It was not until 1943, however, that the process was brought to completion. In that year a measure was passed which authorized the transfer of the residual bishopric endowments to the Commissioners, including the actual residences of the bishops and their grounds, which had been specifically excluded under previous legislation. This marked the final disappearance of the episcopal estates.

Much the same process as was applied to the bishopric estates was followed in the case of the chapter estates. The only difference was that, in the case of the chapter estates, the Commissioners agreed to provide each chapter with an annual income equivalent to the amount previously gained from the estate. It would appear at first sight that this arrangement could not bring any real benefit to the Commissioners, but this was not so. The reason lay in the archaic system of land tenure practised by Church-held estates. It was usual to grant leases of

Church land on a virtually perpetual basis. Although the leases were renewed at regular intervals, it was the practice to regrant them at the previous rental on payment by the lessee of an agreed premium. These premiums were regarded by various Church landlords as income. They could never afford to wait until the natural expiry of a lease or to buy out the incumbent, so while the price of rented land rose steadily all about them the Church estates continued to draw what amounted to little more than peppercorn rentals. In this way, it was estimated in 1835, the Church was losing nearly two-thirds of the real income from its lands. When the lands passed into the administration of the Commissioners, this wasteful practice ceased.

Just how effective the new administration of Church lands was to prove is shown by the total income figures for the second half of the nineteenth century. These rose steadily from £147,000 in 1861 to £1,107,000 in 1891. It is true that part of the increase was due to acquisition of new land by the Commissioners, but it has been estimated that under the old system of administration the income accruing to the bishops, chapters and various other ecclesiastical dignitaries would, in 1891, have amounted to only £452,000.

By the turn of the century the Church, as represented by Queen Anne's Bounty and the Ecclesiastical Commissioners, was established as one of the richest landowners in the country. Although it was regarded as rich primarily in agricultural land, its holdings of mineral rights were extensive and its income from coal royalties, particularly in Durham and Northumberland, considerable. Its tithe rentals formed a highly productive source of income and were not abolished until 1936, when the government paid the Church the sum of £70 million as a consideration for their surrender. Above all the urban properties, particularly in London, were booming. Yet all was not well. The Church's income might appear to be great, but when it came to applying it to the purposes for which it was provided the jam appeared to be pretty thin on the bread.

No matter how well the Church might administer its estates to produce the maximum annual income from their resources, it could not keep pace with the calls made upon it. Its capital assets were not enough to render it financially self-sufficient. Moreover, the changing social pattern had resulted in less and less new land being gifted to the Church. The squire and his family might still occupy the front pew each Sunday, and the squire's wife continue to be a tower of strength in supporting the local sale of work, but the custom of patronage in more substantial form had largely lapsed. In seeking to achieve a corporate financial independence, the Church had become perhaps more inde-pendent than it wanted to be.

There were other causes for disquiet. Although the administration of Church funds was on a much sounder footing than ever before, inadequacies were only too apparent. Its agricultural estates, scattered through all the counties of England, provided a vast administrative problem which exposed shortcomings in Church organization, but its London estates presented an even more serious problem. Of these, Paddington was the most striking – and certainly the most notorious – example.

In the great expansion of the metropolis, Paddington had been one of the most fashionable areas. Rich merchants fell over themselves to obtain a town house in the gracious squares and broad terraces which were being built a short carriage ride from the City. As a residential area it appeared to possess every advantage. It was sufficiently close to Mayfair for some of the glamour of that exclusive area to rub off on it, and Hyde Park, which ran along its south edge, was a place where nannies could take their charges for an airing and ladies show themselves off in the fashionable parade which took place each morning in Rotten Row. In addition, the earlier trustees of the Paddington estate had pulled off what was considered to be a fine stroke of business when they managed, in 1851, to lease part of their land to accommodate a terminus for the Great Western Railway, thus providing easy egress for the tenants to their hunting boxes and country houses. Ever mindful of their tenants' convenience, and perhaps with a prescience of things to come, they laid as a condition of the lease that the engines using the station should be required to 'consume their own smoke'. This assurance having been readily given, the Commissioners happily granted the railway a lease of two thousand years at the very satisfactory rental of £2,571 per annum.*

The decline of Paddington as a residential area for the rich middle class can be ascribed to many causes. Other areas were being developed which were to prove even more desirable. The fine houses of Belgrave Square were grander than the grandest of which Paddington could boast, and Kensington gained favour because of the prestige of Kensington Palace, while the river and the village-like atmosphere gave Chelsea a cachet of its own. Perhaps most of all the station, which had been initially such a cause for pride, proved to be the greatest disadvantage to the area. The engines not only failed to consume their own smoke but the noise of the shunting trucks made residence close to the station unbearable. An ever-widening circle round the station was given over to cheap hotels and rooming-houses, giving convenient

* Paddington Station continued to be rented at this sum until 1958, when the Commissioners decided to make the best of a bad job and sold the freehold to the railway for a capital sum of £43,700.

accommodation to the influx of a class of people who were generally regarded as 'undesirable'. Just as surely as King's Cross, Euston and St Pancras destroyed Bloomsbury as a fashionable district, and Victoria created the slums of Pimlico, so the canker of Paddington spread, until to live 'north of the Park' was as socially disastrous in London as to live on 'the wrong side of the tracks' in America.

The fall from fashion of Paddington created a problem for the Ecclesiastical Commissioners, which was not capable of any immediate solution. In their first flush of enthusiasm the Paddington estate trustees had granted leases on most of their properties for periods up to two thousand years, a headache which the Ecclesiastical Commission inherited. It is perhaps to be accused of hindsight to say that the terms of the leases should have been tied up more tightly. The fact remains that they had been granted in the loosest possible terms. There was virtually no misdemeanour which a tenant could commit which could result in a termination of his tenancy, and sub-lessees were quick to take advantage of the fact. Widows living in genteel poverty in their too large houses had recourse to letting off rooms to anyone who applied for them. More frequently they disposed of their leases altogether to speculators who turned the properties into rooming-houses. In the space of a few years Paddington became one of the most dubious dormitory areas in London. The discouraged Commissioners, finding that their properties were a diminishing asset, were reluctant to spend money on their upkeep, which speeded the decline of the area: the peeling stucco fronts of the houses soon became familiar evidence of the general decay.

Perhaps even more serious was the effect of all this on what, in modern advertising parlance, would be known as the 'brand image' of the Church. As its financial interest in the area was well known, it was often remarked that the Church 'owned all the brothels in London'. For the Commissioners, the wages of sin became a bad joke. Even without this often repeated slur, the general impression was that the properties owned by the Church were largely slums and that the Church was a bad landlord. Like most slanders, it was wide of the mark. Not only did it ignore the high reputation the Church held as an agricultural landlord, but it took no account of the excellently administered estates it owned in other areas such as Kensington, Chelsea and Hampstead.

The latest and final step to be taken by the Church in the long process of setting its financial affairs in order took place in 1948. In that year, Queen Anne's Bounty and the Commissioners were joined into one body, and emerged as the Church Commissioners for England. This was a move which gave them a completely new administrative machinery, the result of an intensive process of self-analysis.

The Church had always shown a marked uneasiness with regard to its own money. The seeming contradiction of its great wealth and the poverty of its clergy embarrassed it. It found it hard to reconcile the financial power it wielded in one hand with the holding of the beggar's bowl in the other. The teaching of the Bible – that it is easier for a camel to go through the eye of a needle than it is for a rich man to enter into the Kingdom of God – made a considerable section of the Church feel guilty. The setting up of the Church Commissioners for England was a final acceptance of the fact that the Church could not contract out of an involvement in worldly affairs; but that this step was accompanied by a new, and, on the whole, welcome frankness about its financial dealings did little to appease its critics. 'Years ago,' complained one of the bishops, 'the cry went round: the Church is inefficient. Now that the Church has appointed competent men to put its house in order, the cry goes up: the Church is money-grubbing.'

In setting up the new Commissioners, the Church gave recognition to the fact that its affairs had grown too complex to be handled by other than the most highly qualified professional men. At first sight, the Commissioners would appear to be an unwieldy body headed by the Archbishop of Canterbury, supported by the Archbishop of York and all the diocesan bishops. Another twenty-five members, of whom over half are clerics, are appointed by the Church Assembly, four are nominated by the Queen, two by the Aldermen of the City of London, and one each by the Vice-Chancellors of Oxford and Cambridge. In addition there are twelve ex-officio members varying from the Chancellor of the Exchequer and the Lord Chief Justice to the Lord Mayor of York.

The main work of administering the financial complex, however, is in the hands of a streamlined Assets Committee headed, as chairman, by the First Commissioner, and a deputy chairman who is Second Commissioner and a senior permanent official of the Crown Estate Office. They are aided by up to six other Commissioners who between them bring expert knowledge and experience relevant to running the estate in all its different aspects.

Perhaps one of the most welcome and effective developments over recent years has been the increasing realization that the most effective way to counter adverse criticism is by giving the maximum exposure of their activities. This is evidenced in particular by the annual publication of the Commissioners' report and accounts, which could well serve as a model for even those giant corporations who have long realized the value of the annual report as an act of public relations. They publish simple-to-understand pamphlets on such old bones of contention and suspicion as clergy pay, pastoral reorganization and so on. In addition the Commissioners themselves undertake speaking tours, mainly to deanery synods and the like. Not so many years ago this attitude to the value of public relations would have been unthinkable.

The organization required to manage the Church empire has its headquarters at No. 1 Millbank, close to Church House where the Church Assembly meets, but appropriately close, also, to the House of Commons, from whom their power also stems. A staff of about four hundred are involved in the intricacies of administration, but of these only about a dozen are high-ranking executives, each wielding at least as much power as the property tycoons and heads of financial houses with whom they have daily dealings. As their function diverges somewhat from the spiritual administration of the Church they have their own public relations officer to interpret their actions and policies to the public. As one senior official remarks: 'When anybody quotes the camel and the eye of the needle to us, we remind them of the parable of the talents.'

Although the wealth of the Church is traditionally founded on the ownership of land, it is now many years since their financial investment in stocks and shares and urban property has not dwarfed the value of their land holdings. At the end of the financial year 1964–65 the total assets of the Church stood at £318,157,338, of which £190,831,699 represented Stock Exchange investments. Twenty years later their Stock Exchange investments totalled £604,400,000 of which £131 million were in the USA. By contrast their agricultural holdings totalled approximately £220 million, representing an ownership of 172,819 acres. Of these, 165,663 acres were tenanted land, 1,435 'in hand' and 5,721 woodland. In 1984 the total property portfolio of the Church totalled £904,700,000 made up as follows:

	£ million
Offices	382.7
Agriculture	217.2
Residential	169.8
Shops	78.5
Industrial	56.5

Surprisingly, their industrial holdings included £18 million worth of investments in a warehouse distribution complex in Dallas, Texas. Add to these figures Stock Exchange investments in the UK, the USA, Australia and the Far East and it can be seen that the Church's total assets twenty years earlier of £318,200,000 were at £1,630,400,000 in 1984 and continue to rise. Impressive though these figures are, when compared with total assets worldwide of the Grosvenor estates they would almost certainly be dwarfed.

When in the early 1980s the Church Commissioners took a decision to sell 208 farms, it gave rise to a rumour that they were preparing to abandon their traditional role as agricultural landlords. In fact the land was sold as a one-off operation to provide money to finance urban development – a shrewd move, as market trends were to show. The Church continues to take considerable pride in its role as landowner, despite the fact that it shows a relatively low return in terms of net income.

The Church steps easily from the role of city tycoon to that of local landowner. Its attitude to its farming tenants is benign and paternalistic. A comparatively recent innovation has been the holding of dinners for tenants and their wives, at which the local bishop presides and representatives of the administrators from Millbank come down to join the fun. 'A real good do,' is how one of the tenants describes these annual junkets. 'Plenty to eat and drink, short speeches and no fussiness.'

Why should the Church Commissioners persevere with low-return agricultural investment? Partly because this is safe in times of inflation, partly in the interests of diversification, and partly because of its traditional connotations. There is no doubt, also, that most churchmen feel more comfortable wearing their country clothes than their city suits. The feeling is actual as well as metaphorical. The Bishop of Taunton, writing in *The Country Parish Today and Tomorrow*, expressed it thus:

> In the country he can still be a *Persona* – the parson. He can still exercise the kind of ministry which the compilers of the *Ordinal** had in mind, and it is only because so many country parsons have an incorrigibly urban mentality that they fail to realise what a privilege and opportunity this confers. The country congregation, though sometimes disconcertingly small, is often fairly representative of the village. During the week the parson has time to make himself acquainted with the labours of the agricultural part of the congregation, and at such times as harvest he can actually share in them. . . . The country parson can do, without making himself a public spectacle, what many town parsons would like to do – that is, share in the same daily work, think the same thoughts and breathe the same air as many members of his Sunday congregation.

The country parson's integrated role in his community is in direct contrast to the situation of the urban parson, who is still apt to assume the role of missionary in his parish. The conclusion that the whole hierarchy of the Church is to a degree conditioned by this attitude is irresistible, and explains its attitude to its role as landowner. Equally there can be no doubt that the shrewd business brains who direct the Church's financial strategy, together with most other institutional investors today, have the same attitude towards investment in land for completely unsentimental reasons.

* The Priesthood's Book of Rules.

9

The Forests

The largest single landholder in Britain is the Forestry Commission. It was set up by a grant of money by Parliament in 1919 as a result of the Acland Report, and in the first year of its existence took over the administration of the forest lands belonging to the Crown Estates, notably the Forest of Dean and the New Forest. Since its early days the Commission has expanded rapidly so that today it controls just over 1.2 million hectares, a slightly smaller total than the amount of afforested land in the hands of private landowners.

Just the same, Britain is one of the poorest countries in terms of timber resources in western Europe with 9 per cent of land devoted to forestry. This represents only around 10 per cent of our national requirement, so 90 per cent has to be imported. Although the Government, immediately following the First World War, showed their awareness of the critically vulnerable state of our timber reserves by establishing the Forestry Commission, it was not until after the Second World War that any determined effort was made to enlist the private landowners into a planned expansion of our forestry resources. This was achieved by offering the inducement of substantial taxation advantages. Today these measures are increasingly under emotive attack by critics who see them purely as a dodge whereby the rich can achieve estate duty exemption at the expense of despoiling the countryside. It has, in fact, proved a successful means of reversing a trend which threatened a serious imbalance in the use of our land resources. The landowners' historical record with regard to afforestation had been an ambivalent one – perhaps understandably.

The vast forests which once covered much of the countryside had little appeal for the established landowner. They harboured his enemies and made it difficult for him to hunt his game. Although the timber they produced was essential for the building of his house, as well as to keep it warm and enable him to cook his food, the forests also occupied areas which could be more productively used as farmland. With the growing need for more and more agricultural land, and the abnormal demand for timber, particularly hardwood, created by successive foreign wars, the once great forests of Britain progressively declined.

The purpose for which timber was used altered with the passing of time. Whilst improved communications brought the blessing of cheap coal to replace wood as fuel, the need of wood for pit props in the mines increased in proportion. When timber was no longer required to build wooden-walled ships, the population explosion created a new demand for building material. The First World War saw an unprecedented ravaging of home resources so that, when peace came, Britain was faced with a serious wood famine which was aggravated by the Second World War.

The fact that much attention had been paid historically by landowners to cutting their timber and little to replanting it must be put down partly to economic necessity and partly to an atavistic feeling that large areas of timber were inimical to good husbandry. It is true that many landowners liked to plant their parklands with oak, elm and ash to beautify the view, and that at the time of the enclosures much hedgerow timber was planted with an eye to its future commercial value; but planned afforestation as it is understood today was virtually non-existent.

There were exceptions to this generalization, notably in Scotland, where some of the biggest landowners showed themselves to be in advance of their times in their attitude. One of the pioneers was the fourth Duke of Atholl, who introduced the larch to Scotland with notable success. The Duke was tireless in his advocacy of tree-planting and he presented a gold medal to his kinsman, James Farquharson of Invercauld, in recognition of his achievement in planting no fewer than 14 million trees on his estate. In his lifetime Farquharson planted almost 20 million trees, many of which still survive. He was not only an indefatigable forester but he had an eye for beauty, planning the layout of his forests with the taste of a Capability Brown but on a much grander scale. Alas, the execution of his designs did not always come up to his expectations, so that little evidence of the master plan remains, although both the Atholl and Farquharson estates have continued to maintain the tradition of good forest management to the present day.

But by no means all the Scottish landowners were sylviculturists. While Farquharson planted, Grant of Rothiemurchus on the other side of the Grampians was cutting his two-hundred-year-old timber as fast as he could to pay his debts, and there were many others. In more recent times, the eleventh Marquis of Huntly (1847–1937) was a great feller of timber. His desperate financial state forced him to denude much of his once vast Aberdeenshire estates before finally selling them. In the end timber as a source of ready cash became an obsession with him. Once, in the last years of his life, when he was staying with a friend who had a well-wooded park (all his own timber had long since gone) a visitor called at the house one morning and asked for him. The host watched with growing curiosity as the two men paced the grounds together. It was only some days after the Marquis had left that it was discovered that he had been soliciting an offer for all his host's standing timber!

The felling of private timber became, in the eighteenth and nineteenth centuries, the most commonly accepted method of getting out of debt. The impoverished Duke of Marlborough was anxious to cut all the trees at Blenheim and had to be restrained by the Court of Chancery, whose job it was to preserve the amenities of the estate. Others found it a convenient way of paying for their children's education, or to meet other financial emergencies. John Byng, whose journals are an interesting record of rural England at the end of the eighteenth century, notes that Lord Abingdon had felled all of the fine timber at Rycote Park, the Duke of Rutland had done the same at Haddon, and at Woburn he was 'shock'd and surprised to see that the axe had been most busy'. At one felling, the Duke of Bedford had chopped down a thousand trees in one avenue. Byng also remarks on 'Mr Fly's ground at Aston, who like most gentlemen of this, and other countries, fell their oak; they think they make amends by planting some larches and Scotch fir, proper ornaments for a desert.'

The record of the smaller landowners was no better. Anxious to reimburse themselves as soon as possible for the capital outlay on enclosing their land, many of them pollarded their trees too early, which not only destroyed their natural beauty but also spoiled the timber. Many others, with the purpose of benefiting from their timber in their own lifetime, planted ash, for, as Cobbett remarks: 'Ash will grow anywhere . . . in hedge-rows, in plantations, everywhere ash is fine . . . it is timber for the wheel-wright at the age of twenty years or less.' The farmers soon found, on the other hand, that the ash is the greediest of all trees, taking all the sustenance out of the ground as far as its roots will spread; and no cattle will graze where its leaves lie. The result was that much of the ash was cut before its time. The elm, by contrast, is not a greedy tree and produces readily saleable timber, which was in great demand in the old days for use underwater. Because of its natural resistance to rot it was widely used for the old city drains, for ships' timbers below the waterline, and for the construction of the Duke of Bridgewater's canals. The 'elm disease' which has ravaged the species up and down the country over the past few years has indeed been a tragedy for one of the most beautiful as well as useful of our indigenous trees. The oak was not popular with many people because of its slow rate of growth, for it was only the most enlightened of landowners who looked beyond the span of their own lifetime. That they were largely also the great landowning families, who looked upon their possessions as a trust held for their children, is evidenced by the fact that most of our finest timber today is to be found in the parks of our historic houses.

It is easy at this distance in time to blame the landowners, who had complete control over one of our greatest natural resources, for their haphazard attitude towards it. At the same time it should be stated that their record was not universally bad. It was privately owned woodlands which met the vast demands for wood during the world wars. By the end of the Second World War all the best timber had either been voluntarily cut or compulsorily purchased at very low controlled prices, and it is only now that we are beginning to recover from this devastation. It must also be said in favour of the landowners, particularly in more recent times, that many showed enthusiasm for experimental work such as the growing of exotic conifers. It was as a result of this work that the Forestry Commission was subsequently able to assess the value of such useful trees as the Sitka spruce, Douglas fir, Norway spruce, Japanese larch, Corsican pine and so on. The landowners, it should be said, had very little official encouragement following the Acts of Enclosure. Britain was leading Europe in agricultural expertise, as she was in industrial development, and even the best landowners were obsessed with improving their farmlands at the expense of all else. There were few, least of all in Government circles, who could foresee a time when the conservation of our timber resources would become a matter of such economic and strategic importance as it is today. In consequence, the timber trade in this country had for many years been organized for imports, so that between the wars the demand for home-grown timber was very limited: planting was not a financially attractive proposition.

Before examining the efforts being made in the present to rectify the sins and omissions of the past, it is interesting to look briefly at the whole question of timber-growing on a much wider basis. Since time began, the pattern of pushing back the forest frontiers has been followed all over the world. Much of the desert area on the world's surface was once highly productive land, supporting a prosperous community with a high standard of living. When the forest became exhausted the land became barren, providing the barest living for its inhabitants, so that their civilization collapsed. That a thousand million of the world's inhabitants are today living at a bare level of subsistence is largely due to the disappearance of the forests, which once provided the necessary balance to make their lands productive. The land flowing with milk and honey of biblical times was no myth. It was once a well-forested area; today it is a stony desert.

Though this sounds rather dramatic, it is no less than the truth, for it is an ecological fact that a proper balance between forested and agricultural land is necessary for fertility, because without trees land not only becomes less fertile but erodes. Today it is generally accepted that the optimum ratio is 30 per cent forested land to 70 per cent agricultural.

Only in very recent times has there been an awakening to the realization that wood is one of the single most valuable commodities known to man, and, even more recently, that there has been any scientific research into the best ways of utilizing it. The Scandinavian countries accept it as the basis of their economy and lead the world in wood technology. As long ago as the mid-1930s Nazi Germany realized its importance as a sinew of war, and made strenuous and partially successful efforts to control the European wood market. Their vast reserves of wood pulp enabled them to be in a far better economic state at the end of the war than would otherwise have been possible. America, by contrast, is profligate in the use of her considerable timber resources. Forest management is not nearly so well understood there as it is in Europe, and millions of acres of what was once magnificent primeval forest have become idle land.

Although Europe leads the world in sylviculture, the utilization of cut timber is only beginning to be understood. It is estimated that for every four trees that are felled, only the equivalent of one tree is used. The rest is wasted. Yet the number of by-products which can be manufactured from the wastage is impressive. They vary from motor fuel to cattle feed and even food fit for human consumption. The chemical capacities of cellulose and lignin, which are produced by all trees, open up a vast field of new research, whilst the chemical properties of individual trees are continually being discovered.

Egon Glesinger, one of the world authorities on wood, in his book *The Coming Age of Wood*, envisages it as a new basis for a world economy. He puts forward impressive arguments for a re-afforestation programme which would have the effect of raising the standard of living throughout the world and particularly in the great denuded areas in the East. At the same time he predicts that, without planned forest management on a global basis, we may well face a world famine by the end of the century. It is true that there are still 5,000 million acres of virgin wood in regions of Africa, Latin America, Alaska, Manchuria and Siberia, but so great is the demand for wood and wood products that even this great reserve can become exhausted. If timber is treated as any other crop, however, to be harvested and replaced systematically, it is a commodity which is virtually inexhaustible. But little comfort can be derived from an estimated statistic that international timber and food companies are cutting timber at the rate of *50 acres a minute* without feeling any obligation to replant the areas they are systematically devastating.

It is against this background that we must consider the utilization
of land for forestry in this country. It has been accepted that, while we
can never produce enough timber to supply our needs, it is only
common sense that efforts should be made to strive towards greater
productivity.

This is not a view which is by any means universally held in the
political arena. One senior member of a past Government gave it as his
view that there was no point in planting trees when there was no future
for home-grown timber, and there are many others who, either from
political bias or from basic hostility to everything to do with private
ownership, view with suspicion the various financial incentives given to
landowners to plant timber. Others resent the very considerable
amount of Government money being invested in state-owned forests.

By contrast the Timber Growers' Association, who operate in the
private sector, question the wisdom of any cutback in the planting
programme: 'We do not believe it can be sensible to continue to spend
year after year on buying timber products from abroad, a sum which is
about equivalent *annually* to the total expenditure by Governments over
the last fifty years.' Of all the EEC countries only Ireland and the
Netherlands are worse off with regard to timber resources. The forecast
that the price of timber will have risen by 30 per cent (in excess of
inflation) by the year 2000 makes the picture look gloomy indeed.

One of the less informed outbursts of public indignation over what
amounts to the subsidizing of afforestation in the private sector
occurred in 1986 when a well-known television personality was
discovered to have made a substantial investment in land consisting of
barren moorland and bog in the north of Scotland, on which he has
planted trees. Nobody would seek to claim that an investment of this
sort by Mr Terry Wogan or anyone else has been made for altruistic
reasons. The indignation is, however, entirely misplaced, fuelled as it is
by no doubt well-meaning conservationists whose ambition in this
instance seems to be to conserve a desert – or rather a bog.

Nothing has affected the quality of life in Scotland more adversely
than its progressive deforestation, and of no part of Scotland is this
more true than in the northerly counties, known as the crofting
counties. Much has been made of the callousness of the lairds at the
beginning of the nineteenth-century Clearances, whereby the tenants
were removed from their crofts to make way for sheep. This is another
emotive issue which has become somewhat clouded with the passage of
time. It is certainly true that the agents for the first Duke of Sutherland,
who is generally cast as the leading villain of the piece largely on
account of his being by far the largest landowner of his time, showed
appalling insensitivity to a group of men who would rather starve in

familiar surroundings than be forced to leave them. In fact the Duke's intentions were well-meaning enough – feeling that his tenants, whom he regarded as his personal chattels, would have a better life employed in coastal industries such as fishing, he merely moved them there; he did not, as is popularly supposed, force them to emigrate. In fact when the Highland Clearances were at their height the population of Sutherland showed an increase rather than a decline. Nor did the clearing of the hill land for sheep farming reap, in most cases, rich profits. Sheep raising, particularly in the very north of Scotland, proved an unprofitable business, and today much of the 'cleared' lands lies barren. The only possible regeneration of these areas lies in forestry. The Acts of Enclosure which were being enacted at the same time in England were, in many cases, far more injurious to the peasantry, but at least led to a vastly more profitable use of the land from which they had been driven out.

The Forestry Commission itself does not normally invoke arbitrary powers. Like other Civil Service departments concerned with land utilization, it has a right of compulsory purchase but prefers to compete for its land in the open market. Thus it frequently arises that, when negotiating for an area of land suitable for development as a forest, the Commission is put in the position of having to buy considerable acreages of other land as well which is not suitable for the main purpose. A landowner disposing of an estate is often unwilling to break it up into component parts and sell his agricultural land separately from his woodland. As a result the Commission has, with the passing of the years, become one of the largest holders of agricultural land in the country – perhaps the largest. Sometimes it is able to sell off the farmlands at a later date, but most of it is leased off, or in some cases farmed by the Commission itself.

An even greater embarrassment to the Forestry Commission is the amount of land it is forced to buy which has no commercial value whatsoever. This is most frequently the case in Scotland, where the barren hillsides make ideal land for forestry development. At the same time much of the available hillside forms the foot slopes of mountains whose peaks rise far above the tree line. It is considered uneconomic in this country to plant trees higher than 2,000 feet above sea level; 1,600 feet is probably a more practical level. Nobody is willing to sell the lower slopes of a mountain only, so the Commission has been forced to acquire much high, barren land which it has no possible use for, except possibly to let for deer stalking. Thus out of a total of 760,000 hectares which the Commission controls in Scotland, only 550,000 hectares are actually suitable for planting. The balance is made up in the main of 93,500 hectares of farm or grazing land, and another 107,000 hectares which is unplantable. The proportion of waste land in England is, of course, very much smaller.

With this vast amount of land at their disposal the Forestry Commissioners have a clear responsibility to ensure that the maximum opportunities for open-air recreation are available to the public, subject always to the prime necessity of producing timber. It is a responsibility which the Commission takes seriously, although it does not always manage to escape criticism. The dangers from fire or of damage to small trees are obvious factors which preclude the use of large areas by the public, but the establishment of Forest Parks – of which there are seven – has demonstrated the immense demand which exists for proper facilities for open-air recreation. Last year over 1,200,000 campers and caravanners used the Commission's camp sites. In addition, the Commissioners have interested themselves in a diversity of enterprises, from providing grazing land for the first herd of reindeer in this country to giving facilities for adventure-training courses. In view of their efforts to accommodate the public need for recreation, they resent the recent suggestion that the New Forest, long a favourite beauty spot, should be removed from their jurisdiction and placed under the care of a specially constituted authority.

When a Labour Government was returned to power in 1945 it gave its general blessing to a continued policy of expansion, with an ultimate figure of 5 million acres of state forest as a possible objective. It was a figure which, one senior forestry official remarks, was 'snatched out of the air'. Today a figure of 7 million acres is more commonly mentioned, but there is no certainty that it is capable of achievement. All successive Governments have adopted some sort of national forestry policy, the most recent of which arises from a comprehensive review which was carried out in 1979–80. Following this a statement was made on 10 December 1980 by Mr George Younger, then Secretary of State for Scotland, which amply demonstrated the Government's awareness of the problems involved and of the importance of forestry to the national economy.

> With the projected rise in demand for timber into the next century and with the world's forests likely to come under increasing pressure, the Government believe that long-term confidence in both forestry and wood-processing industries in this country is fully justified. We look for a steadily increasing proportion of our requirements of timber to come from our own resources. A continuing expansion of forestry is in the national interest, both to reduce our dependence on imported wood in the long term and to provide continued employment in forestry and associated industries.
>
> Recent difficulties in the pulp and paper sector, which represents only one-eighth of the market for wood grown in this country, do not change that

conclusion. Forest owners have adjusted to the changed markets. Export opportunities in Europe for small roundwood are being successfully exploited. Looking further ahead, our industries, with the more advanced processes being developed in this country, are expected to be capable of absorbing the rising production from our existing forests, and of enlarging their present 9 per cent share of the home market.

There are still plenty of problems. The demand from the sheep farmers for more and more land are making the market for suitable land for forestry more competitive. Recently the Commission has only been able to buy land in some areas because of the difficulty in finding shepherds. Nor are the Commission's own labour problems always easy. Today it employs a labour force of almost 40,000 in its forests, bringing much-needed employment to remote country areas, but the labour drift from these areas is becoming more pronounced. On the other hand, there is evidence that a new prosperity for the timber industry is in sight. The establishment by the big paper corporations of large processing plants in various parts of the country foreshadows better utilization of timber and higher productivity. It is true that all our timber production put together could not keep one of the giant Finnish mills in production, but it is still a step in the right direction.

The part played by the private landowners in maintaining timber production has always been important, although it is only within recent years that any attempt has been made to coordinate their efforts, or any real assistance offered them by the state. Today the assistance is both real and realistic, so that, particularly on the larger estates, forestry plays an important part in the economy of the whole.

To undertake the task of explaining the way in which the landowner benefits from planting trees is fraught with pitfalls and difficulties, for the financial details vary widely from case to case. It is, however, such an important aspect of modern estate management that some effort must be made to do so. Nor is the task made any easier by the reluctance of many estate owners to discuss their forestry projects in detail. This is an attitude which springs from the criticisms of Government financial policy *vis-à-vis* the timber grower. Some of the more uninformed opinion has not stopped short of describing the benefits offered by successive governments as tax 'fiddles' or at best 'concessions'; the timber growers prefer to refer to them as 'reliefs'. The general climate of opinion has not been helped by the activities of city tycoons, who have been quick to see personal advantages, from an estate duty and tax point of view, in investment in forest land. The difference in sympathy for a professional landowner trying to make his estate pay its way, and a financier with no interest in the land other than gaining a personal benefit out of the same operation, is readily understandable. In fact, there are probably fewer in the latter category than is generally imagined, but their activities have been widely noticed.

Although the necessity of giving Government support to timber growing has been recognized since before the last war, it was only in 1947 that the present pattern of operations was introduced. One of the more important steps taken in that year was the launching of the dedication scheme. Under this arrangement landowners were invited to 'dedicate' land to forestry, which meant giving an undertaking that the landowner and his heirs would use the land for no purpose other than the growing of timber, and this to be done under an agreed plan with the supervision of a skilled forester. In return, the landowner became eligible for certain grants. The dedication scheme was closed to new applicants in 1981 and was superseded by the Forestry Grants Scheme, which works in a rather less complicated way and basically amounts to a Government grant of 25 per cent of net approved expenditure.

If this was the only encouragement given to private landowners to plant timber it is likely that very few acres indeed would be planted. There are, however, two other main factors to be taken into consideration. The first is that when an estate is valued for probate, standing timber is exempted. This is reasonable enough, for it is not an immediately realizable asset, and to include it might well cripple the whole estate and result in its having to be broken up. The duty only becomes payable when the asset is realized, which in most cases is to the considerable advantage of the heirs of the original planter.

The second factor is even more important. This is the provision that forest land may be planted under Schedule D of the Income Tax return, which means that effectively the whole cost of planting can be claimed against tax. For someone with a high rate of income tax this is obviously a great advantage, for it means that a high proportion of his investment is actually paid for by the state. At the same time, if the ownership of the land changes hands, for example, on the death of the owner, all forest land is reclassified for income tax purposes as being under Schedule B, and assessed not at the developed value of the land, but at its original value before planting, which might be as low as five shillings per acre.

Thus a well-forested estate is a protection against inflation and against crippling death duties, as well as being the means of preserving a valuable asset from one generation to the next. The support given by successive Governments, both Conservative and Labour, to these measures, is a demonstration of the realization in responsible quarters of the pressing need for greater timber reserves in the country.

The response from the traditional landowners to the dedication scheme was very great. Within ten years of its adoption no fewer than

2,750 estates had adopted it, involving over 830,000 acres of woodland. Today, under the present system of grants and tax relief, much of the impetus for the afforestation of land has come from investors in the City and organizations like Timber Growers (UK) Ltd, who run a highly efficient service which gives advice to private investors.

Of the traditional landowners, probably the greatest afforestation has been carried out by the Earl of Seafield, with between 40,000 and 50,000 acres on his Scottish estates – an area equivalent to all the Forestry Commission woodlands in the south of England if the New Forest is excluded. The Scottish lairds have been historically the greatest timber growers, and so they have remained to the present day. The Duke of Buccleuch has large acreages in the Lowlands; so has his neighbour Lord Home of The Hirzel. On the Queen's private estates on Deeside, a great deal of forestry is being undertaken after years of inactivity, and wide areas of the west and north are taken up with private forest land, with the Duke of Atholl, the Earl of Moray and the Earl of Cawdor amongst the largest owners.

In England, one of the most active of all the big landowners is the Earl of Bradford at Weston Park in Shropshire, who is carrying on the tradition of his father as president of the Timber Growers' Organization. He is closely followed, both in enthusiasm and number of acres, by the Earl of Lonsdale, who has taken a step forward in private enterprise by installing his own electronic sawmill in Cumberland, on the site of what was once his private railway station.

There is no doubt that the postwar years have seen advances in the coordination of the forestry industry in this country, as between the state forests, private forestry and the home-grown timber trade. That this should continue to develop in an even more definitive way is essential if the industry is to survive on a profitable basis. The profit motive, which has not always played a big part in the reckonings of the private forest owners in the past, is today as important to them as the profitability of agriculture or any other branch of estate management, and profit can only be assured by improved marketing methods.

Constant research is being carried out into new uses for such materials as steel, concrete and plastics, backed by intensive propaganda for their products by the industries concerned. There is no doubt that the timber trade would benefit enormously from similar activity. In particular, fresh markets must be found for the lower-grade hardwoods. Much of the standing hardwood today is of inferior quality – particularly oak – so that it is not worth the owners' while to clear it. The cost of doing so, together with replanting with more useful species, would be prohibitive – yet it should be done. To develop a market for, say, oak particle board or charcoal is, however, beyond the capabilities of the individual. It can only be achieved by a sustained cooperative effort. Landowners tend to be individualists speaking not with one voice but with many, yet nowhere is the need greater for them to combine in common purpose than in the forestry industry – and to combine not only amongst themselves but to form a true partnership with the Forestry Commission, which is showing considerable initiative in developing new markets.

It is largely on the successful realization of this aim that the landowners' future will depend.

10

The Sporting Estate

The image of the landowner is nowhere more caricatured than in his sporting activities: it is the field in which he is most often criticized by his detractors. Nothing is more infuriating to the envious than the bland assumption by the owner of land that he also has an exclusive right to all the game on his property, or that to own a piece of the bank of a river is also to own the fish.

Foxhunting is criticized for different reasons. It is the chief whipping boy of the anti-blood sports faction, who are becoming even more vociferous in their condemnation of it. As has been remarked elsewhere, the character of foxhunting has changed vastly since the middle of the eighteenth century. Indeed in earlier times hounds were not used for hunting foxes at all, but for the pursuit of hares. It was only after packs like the Quorn and the Brocklesby started to breed a faster type of hound, which could hunt down a fox before it could reach its earth, that foxes became the chief quarry. With the coming of the enclosures, the sport took on a different aspect. The element of jumping was introduced, and it became the fashion for young blades on thoroughbreds to demonstrate their courage by riding hard across country. If this was dangerous, it was also capable of giving rise to situations which were little short of comedy, as the following account, by Lady Elizabeth Grosvenor, of a day with the Belvoir in 1828 demonstrates:

> They hunted from Eastwell – a burst and a longish run. Belgrave [her husband, Lord Grosvenor] rode Amber who pulled and got a cut on his foreleg from a stub. He had Rampion out as a second horse, but as Wilton [his brother] lamed both his horses, he rode him. Belgrave had a fall on Amber in a brook from a man falling before him and strained his leg. Wilton was also in a brook. George Anson had a fall and slid into a lump of black mud. Mr Maxse, in crossing a hand bridge with a stile at the end, got his horse's hind legs fast through the rails and there stuck until some sympathetic friends came to his relief with a hatchet. Worcester, in pulling his horse out of a brook, pulled the bridle out of its mouth on which the horse judiciously set off the wrong way and was no more heard of.

Hunting was always a popular sport with the countryman, whatever his station. The farmers wanted the foxes killed, and the labourers earned many a shilling for their services in opening gates or pointing the way the fox had gone. Towns like Melton owed much of their prosperity to the annual invasion of foxhunting men up from London, and the events of the day were talked over as eagerly in the pubs as a football match is today. Criticism of foxhunting is only of very recent origin.

Shooting, by contrast, has traditionally been surrounded by contention between the landowner and the peasantry, ever since it first became a fashionable sport towards the end of the eighteenth century. The decline of hawking and the rise in popularity of shooting was largely due to the introduction of the new flintlock gun perfected by Joseph Manton. Although the new double-barrelled guns were still muzzle-loaded, which meant that the sportsman had to carry such impedimenta as ramrod, powder flask and horn, they were altogether much more efficient than anything which had gone before. Bags could be attained to compare with a reasonable day's rough shooting nowadays.

The invention of the flintlock had, however, a much more serious effect on the countryside. By making shooting fashionable it also made the preservation of game more desirable, which started a war of attrition between the landowner and the poaching fraternity, the cause of much bitterness and bloodshed for many years. There were few sections of the agricultural community who were not involved in it.

It is hard not to find oneself in sympathy with the offenders against the game laws, which so stringently preserved a monopoly for a privileged few. Under a series of Acts passed in the reign of George III, the killing of game was restricted to owners of land worth £100 a year, or lessees of land worth £150, or persons of a rank not lower than the eldest son of an esquire. Under the Ellenborough Act of 1803, the penalty for a poacher offering armed resistance to his apprehension was death, and by a later Act the penalty for any form of poaching at night was seven years' transportation which was tantamount to transportation for life, as few convicts could ever raise the money for their passage home.

It was also illegal for anyone at all to sell game, with the result that to serve game at table became a prime status symbol. This had the natural effect of creating a lively black market. The newly rich would go to any lengths to procure game so as to demonstrate that they were among the privileged few, and there were few inns of any quality which did not provide by some means or another game for their guests. This circumstance, coupled with the extreme poverty of the farm labourers, made it inevitable that there would always be a large number who would risk the severest penalties to earn a few shillings. Indeed the severity of the penalties resulted in their forming themselves into larger and more desperate gangs determined to resist arrest at any cost. It is not surprising that the peace of the countryside was gravely disturbed. Running fights at night were common occurrences, often with fatal results. 'There is now hardly a jail delivery in which some gamekeeper has not murdered a poacher, or some poacher a gamekeeper,' wrote Sydney Smith.

In the poaching war, the sympathy of the countryside was almost entirely on the side of the poachers and against the landowners. The landowners, secure in the knowledge that the law was on their side, went to inhuman lengths to protect their preserves. The use of the man-trap, which seldom killed a man but could maim him for life, was common. So was the trip gun which, when disturbed, discharged a barrel of buckshot at the intruder; this quite often resulted in the death of an innocent child who had wandered into the woods. The appalling disparity between the condition of a poacher driven by dire poverty to snaring a pheasant, and the immense wellbeing of the privileged landowner, could not but excite the sympathy of the outsider. Just the same it was not until 1831, when nearly a sixth of all criminal convictions in the country were for poaching offences, that the qualifications required to take game were relaxed and the sale of game made legal.

It was only much later in the century, with the invention of the breech-loading sporting gun and prefabricated cartridges, that shooting started to take on the pattern which is familiar today. The driving of birds over guns – known in early days as 'battues' – had been introduced early in the century, but with muzzle-loading guns the bags could not hope to compare with the vast ones obtained with more modern weapons. Even so, some of the bags recorded in the early nineteenth century were surprisingly large. 'Conceive of the game killed at Knowsley [Lord Derby] this year,' wrote Lady Elizabeth Grosvenor in 1826, 'amounting to 27,000 head, but 21,000 being rabbits makes one understand it better.'

For many years after the abolition of the more onerous of the game laws, the attitude of the landowners towards the sporting facilities offered by their estates remained unchanged. Some of the laws, indeed, were preserved in private form. For example, many estate owners continued to insist that no employee or tenant on their estates could own a sporting dog, long after the law which had laid this down had been abolished. It was also generally considered not quite the thing to sell the game which was shot. Some of the larger landowners continued to preserve their amateur status in this respect well into the twentieth century. At the end of each day's shooting the bag would be divided up amongst the guns, and the surplus sent off by rail in boxes to relations and friends all over the country, or delivered to hospitals and other worthy recipients.

By the beginning of this century, shooting had become one of the main preoccupations of the aristocracy and the landed gentry, who vied with one another to produce bigger and bigger bags. Invitations to the best shoots were eagerly sought after, and ability with a gun as generally admired as prowess in the hunting field. The whole trend was given great impetus by Edward VII, himself one of the best shots in the country; his Sandringham estates were run more for the sport they produced than in the interests of the farming tenants.

The dedication of the shooting enthusiasts was quite as remarkable as the size of the bags achieved. Lord Ripon constructed a catapult which fired paper pellets. Armed with this, he would while away his hours of boredom during the close season shooting at flies! Sir Harry Stonor was such an expert shot that he used to shoot with three guns, and often, it is said, achieved the feat of killing six driven grouse out of a single covey. The speed and accuracy required to do this may be realized when it is considered that he would probably have four birds dead in the air at once. Some of the bags shot were of astounding proportions, the most remarkable feat being that of Lord Walsingham, who had 1,070 grouse to his own gun in one day. Five guns at Blenheim, at the end of the last century, accounted for 6,943 rabbits, and a few years later there were 3,937 pheasants shot in one day at Hall Barn in Buckinghamshire. The most recent sporting record was achieved by a Lincolnshire farmer called Nickerson (now Sir Joseph Nickerson) who, with five other guns, killed 2,015 partridges in 1952 – a feat which is unlikely ever to be surpassed, as the partridge is becoming increasingly rare in most parts of the country.

Until the turn of the century, it is probably true to say that there were few large landowners who were concerned with the economics of the sporting rights they owned. They were entirely preoccupied with the sport that their estates offered for themselves and their guests. Nor were they subject to the same pressures that prevail today. The number of people who did not already own land and who had a taste for shooting and fishing was comparatively small, so that a landowner who had greater facilities than he had use for often found difficulty in getting a let. This was particularly true in Scotland, where the estates were generally much bigger than in England, and where the impoverished Highland lairds competed with one another to attract the few rich Europeans and Americans who were beginning to discover the sporting attractions of the country. Even so, many of the finest salmon rivers and grouse moors went untenanted from year to year, and the market for salmon and game was strictly limited. It was common for servants being taken on in a landowning household to stipulate as a condition of employment that they should not be required to eat salmon or venison more than twice a week.

Today the sporting scene has undergone a complete revolution. The demand for the very best fishing and shooting far exceeds the supply, and spiralling rentals have brought a fresh source of income to many estates which would have perished without it. The once unproductive hillsides of Scotland and the north of England now reap a golden harvest, and it is seldom possible to acquire a beat on a salmon river, in spite of the very high rentals which they command. There are few, if any, landowners today who can afford to ignore the commercial aspect of the sporting rights which they own.

There has also been a revolution in the relationship between the landowner and those who earn their living from the land. That this should have taken place progressively with the abolition of the harsh penalties for poaching is not a contradiction in terms. There never was a time when the countryman was 'anti' what are now known generically as blood sports. It was simply the draconian penalties imposed on a man, often driven by sheer poverty to lift a rabbit to help feed his starving family, which fuelled the state of almost open warfare which existed between the haves and the have-nots of England's green and pleasant land. This does not mean that the traditional local poacher who plies his trade wherever there is game to be poached is not still something of a folk hero in most countryside areas, and even stood the odd pint by his arch-enemy the head gamekeeper should they chance to find themselves in the same pub. That is all part of the tradition of tolerance and good humour which is so typically British.

One of the most remarkable aspects of the anti-blood sports lobby is their almost total ignorance of the subject. It is perhaps understandable that the spectacle of a number of rich gentlemen potting away at pheasants, one of our most beautiful native birds, driven over their heads by beaters purely for the fun of the thing should be an emotive issue in the class war. Quite apart from anything else, there is considerably less cruelty in pheasant shooting than in intensive stock farming. If the activists were, for example, to picket slaughterhouses they would at least be consistent.

Grouse shooting is by far the most expensive as well as the most fashionable form of sport, but another source of income which is becoming even more profitable to the Highland lairds is the letting of deer forests. The sport of stalking suffered a decline in the immediate postwar years, but has recently shown a marked revival. From the landowners' point of view this is an admirable trend, for much of the land let for stalking has little other use. The deer forests are too remote to make the grazing of sheep a practical proposition, and are usually too high and rugged for grouse. It is all the more pity, therefore, that some of the mountain tops which could be profitable stalking lets have become sterilized areas, through the planting of forests on the lower slopes which cut off the deer's access to the low ground. Although it is usual nowadays to leave gaps through the plantations, the Forestry Commission in particular must take some of the blame that this happened too frequently in the postwar era.

It is typical of the uninformed criticisms levelled against the landowners that they have been taken to task for the 'farming' of deer largely on the grounds that the land could have been put to more economic use. This is practically never so. Large areas of the north-west of Scotland, such as the Duchess of Westminster's estate at Loch More, have no other use than as deer forests. As it is, the need for stalkers provides welcome employment in those areas where it is most needed. Perhaps the most enthusiastic supporter of the red deer is the Duke of Atholl, who speaks on the subject frequently in the House of Lords. A large portion of his Perthshire estate is only suitable for deer, and in one of the most remote areas he has created a deer sanctuary where they can breed without disturbance. As a result not only does the estate benefit from the letting of the surrounding forests, but an export trade in venison has been built up with Germany, which provides a very considerable revenue every year in addition to letting rentals.

Stalking is let either for a period, as in the case of grouse moors, to one tenant or to a syndicate, who are supplied with a lodge and stalkers, or let for one or two days at a time. Prices have risen steeply in the last few years. On one West Highland estate the rate in the 1950s for a day's stalking, with a jeep and stalker, was £12. Today the same facilities fetch £200 including the price of one stag. It is unusual for the stalking tenant to keep the stag he kills: it remains the property of the proprietor, who markets the deer through one of the several agents who operate in the north. The hinds are later shot by the stalkers on a purely commercial basis and marketed in the same way, so that the farming of deer and their careful conservation results in a real contribution to the economics of a Highland estate.

The rise in popularity of salmon fishing is another aspect of the sporting estate which has greatly benefited the owners. Beats on the great salmon rivers of Scotland and England change hands for high prices, if a willing seller can be found – which is comparatively rare – and rentals are proportionately high, although they vary considerably from river to river and according to the time of year. On such rivers as the famous Tweed in the Scottish Borders rentals have in recent years spiralled to unprecedented heights. The Tweed is noted for its autumn run of fish, so whilst a beat in the spring for six rods might cost in the region of £1,000 a week, in the autumn on, for example, Junction Pool at Kelso, the first week in October costs around £5,000 and by the last week in November the price will have risen to over £8,000.

Of course beats, particularly those in the far north in Sutherland, although they are ever more in demand, can be had for very much less (although subject to seasonal peaks) with June and July offering the best chance of success. Indeed, in the far north particularly it is not unusual for a considerable part of the rental to be paid for by the sale of fish, and it is by no means unknown for a lucky speculator to make a profit if the run of fish is exceptionally good. On the other hand, through lack of water or any of a number of other reasons, he might hit a bad patch and be heavily out of pocket. Either way it does not matter to the owner of the water, who is assured of his rental come what may.

While the tenant has to pay a high price to enjoy his sport, it must not be thought that this is net profit to the landowner. He has to pay to have his property keepered all the year round; he must maintain his shooting lodges, keep his moors drained and his butts in good repair, or in the case of a pheasant shoot stock his coverts and feed his winter stock. Thus a middle-priced moor might absorb 50 per cent of the rental in running costs. Pheasant shoots are particularly costly, because of the constant need to restock and the higher price of labour; it is estimated that it costs almost £15 to put a bird over the guns. A good pheasant shoot will have a stock of several thousand birds.

At the same time, sporting rights are certainly playing an increasingly important part in balancing budgets on many estates. Invercauld, for instance, in the centre of Scotland, which has been the ancestral home of the Farquharsons for hundreds of years and which extends to over 100,000 acres, would be unlikely to survive in the modern world without the benefit of its twenty-four miles of the River Dee, which is one of the most highly prized rivers in Scotland, and its extensive grouse moors.

The value of sporting rights may be judged by the sale three years ago of a Yorkshire grouse moor – admittedly one of the finest in the country – for a mind-boggling sum said to be in the region of £2 million. It was bought by Sheik Al Maktoum who, unusually for very rich Arabs, who prefer to invest in bricks and mortar, already has considerable land holdings in both England and Scotland. Like his other sporting properties the Sheik bought Bolihope for his personal enjoyment – a luxury that very few landowners can afford. He has recently been reported as having installed a refrigeration plant on his moor so that the day's bag, in 1987 said to be as high as 700 brace, can be instantly frozen. This is a further refinement which only the richest could afford – although what the Sheik does with this large number of frozen grouse is a matter for conjecture.

The high value of sporting land, which has saved many estates from dissolution, the amount of seasonal employment which it creates in the more remote regions, and the increasing availability of sporting facilities to those able to afford to pay for them, do not, however, supply a complete answer to critics who maintain that access to the countryside should be made available to all, and that the day of private ownership of sporting rights is past. The answer lies somewhere between the extremists in both camps. The left-wing iconoclast, who maintains that there should be freedom for all to shoot or fish where they please, and to whom preservation in any form is anathema, is far removed from the realities of the situation. Equally, there are landowners who take preservation to such lengths as to do a disservice to their own cause.

The bigger the landowner, the greater his responsibility to see that his land is used to the best advantage by the largest number of people. There are few who would argue that the owner of a small agricultural estate, a single stretch of river or a small acreage of hill land should not be able to enjoy the sporting amenities for himself and his friends. They are as inalienable to him as his rights under any other aspect of landownership. The really large landowner is in a different position. So far as sporting rights are concerned, he must consider how far he can allow organized access without it detracting from his main purpose, which is to achieve the highest productivity of which his land is capable.

That sporting rights are a desirable amenity is undoubted, but it must be remembered that without careful preservation much of the amenity would not exist. The good-natured farmer who allows anyone to shoot at will over his land, and does nothing to preserve his stocks, will soon find that there is nothing left to shoot. The pheasant, the most common of all our gamebirds, owes its very existence to the fact that it has been carefully preserved and that many hundreds of thousands of birds are bred every year to keep up stocks. Equally, if the coveys of grouse are not broken up by shooting, and young heather provided for them to feed on by systematic burning, they will contract disease and their numbers will decline; the control of vermin is also essential to the survival of all gamebirds. These are expenses which traditionally come out of the landowner's pocket. If he invests in improving his sporting amenities he is surely entitled to make what profit he can from his enterprise. That this should result in the rationing of the commodity by price is no more deplorable than the fact that Dover sole costs more than herring.

On the other hand there are aspects of sporting facilities where much more can be done by the big landowners. Many hundreds of lochs in Scotland are neither fished by their owners nor open to the public. This is all the more to be deplored because most Scottish lochs thrive on being fished hard. If they are not, the trout either contract worm or reach a stage when there are too many fish for the food available so that they never grow to any size. At the same time the demand for trout fishing on lochs or rivers is constantly increasing. Busloads of workers from the industrial towns, and particularly from the mining areas, are prepared to drive hundreds of miles over the weekend to find some sport. If facilities are not available, it is not unknown for them to take over a stretch of river for the day and resist any attempt to move them.

Equally local sportsmen, deprived of any facilities, take to poaching, which generates bad feeling between the landowner and the rest of the community. Legislation introducing stiffer penalties for the taking of salmon and deer has helped to control the organized poaching by city gangs which was becoming a national scandal. However, the return from, for example, the use of monofil netting for salmon off the estuaries of some of our richest rivers, like the Tweed and the Tay, has rendered these penalties negligible.

The more enlightened landowners are finding that it is good policy to provide what facilities they can. One large estate owner in the north, who was considerably troubled by poachers, solved his problem by inviting the most hardened poacher to form a fishing club, and provided two lochs and a stretch of river for the purpose. It proved highly successful. The club members themselves contributed to the restocking of the water and the landowner's private rights were assiduously respected.

The practice of forming fishing clubs for the benefit of the community is becoming more widespread, with landowners like the Duke of Atholl leading the way. Other owners, like the Earl of Lonsdale, encourage out-of-season activities, like pigeon shooting clubs, which have the double virtue of providing sport for the members and controlling the numbers of pigeons. Most of the bigger landlords, from the Duke of Buccleuch downwards, let large portions of their estates either to individuals or to sporting syndicates, but there are others, particularly amongst the newer of the land aristocracy, who make little or no contribution to solving the problem.

The fact remains that the sporting amenities in this country are better and more varied than almost anywhere else in the world and are a national asset. In America, where the private landowners have not been allowed to conserve their sporting rights, game is so scarce as to be negligible, in spite of the high prices which are paid for licences. The result is that wealthy Americans think nothing of adding the cost of a transatlantic trip to the large sums they pay to join in sporting syndicates in this country, and return year after year, together with their Continental counterparts, as satisfied customers. So great is the annual influx of sporting wealth to the remote northern counties of Scotland that it is estimated to earn 98 per cent of the rates.

Today, the picture of the sporting landowner is a vastly different one from that which prevailed in the last century, although the memory lingers on. Whether through economic pressure or a genuine change of heart, many of the old barriers have been broken down. In most instances the sporting estate is no longer one rich man's plaything, but a viable economic proposition to be managed in the same way as agriculture, forestry or any other aspect of running an estate. That this should result in its enjoyment by a greater number of people is in keeping with the spirit of the times.

There is, however, one further aspect of the controversy which appears to surround the use of land for the purposes of sport which it is appropriate to air in discussing the future of the sporting estate. There is today an increasingly strong lobby pressing for legislation to make unrestricted access to common land the right of every member of the public. This is to misunderstand completely the meaning of the term 'common land'. Common land is in fact almost always privately owned, but subject to certain rights vested in others who are registered under the Common Registration Act of 1965 as 'commoners'; they are usually farmers, and their rights over the land limited to its use for agricultural purposes. This multiple use of land arises out of a movement which started about a hundred years ago as a reaction to the progressive enclosing of common lands under private Acts of Enclosure as described in Chapter 2. It was often directed very properly at the preservation of urban commons, to give town dwellers in the expanding industrial areas access to fresh air and exercise.

A great deal of the common land registered today is also subject to the sporting rights being reserved to the owner. At the same time this does not lessen the usefulness of common land as areas where plants and other wildlife can be preserved rather in the way that nature reserves are designed for these purposes with strictly limited public access. Those most vociferous in agitating for the restriction on access to common lands to be lifted are often motivated by considerations not entirely concerned with the public good. The more ferocious opponents of blood sports see the retention of sporting rights by the owner of common land as a totally unwarranted extension of privilege, and would happily use legal right of access to such lands to disturb the rights of the owner; and, of course, what are generically known as blood sports provide a far more emotive issue than agriculture. That to disturb grouse or, for that matter, any other species of birds during the breeding season would eventually lead to the extinction of the species does not weigh heavily with the extremists.

Recently the Common Land Forum has been set up by the Countryside Commission in which both owners and 'commoners', along with other representative bodies, have a voice. The earliest reports suggest that a workable formula may be found which can offer a sensible solution to a problem which has been bedevilled by misunderstanding and misrepresentation of the real issues involved.

11

The United States of America

It might be instructive as a postscript to the previous chapter to examine briefly landownership in the USA. Americans like to regard their country primarily as an agricultural one and are even more paranoid about who owns what than are European countries, and particularly paranoid about any suggestion that foreign interests are buying up their farmland.

As early as the late eighteenth century and well into the nineteenth, individual states were passing laws to curtail or prevent foreigners buying land in the USA – measures which were largely aimed at discouraging further immigration. Wyoming seems to have been the exception. In the late nineteenth century many of the big English landowners invested heavily in the cattle lands. Even Queen Victoria herself, so it was rumoured, was amongst the aristocrats to cash in on the golden prospects offered by cattle ranching. At one time more of the developing state of Wyoming was owned by armchair ranchers in Britain than by American pioneers. The hopes of vast fortunes for the British and Anglo–American companies shrivelled and died in the phenomenally severe winters of 1878 and 1880, when the starving cattle died in their hundreds of thousands and the emaciated survivors finished up in the slaughterhouses of Chicago, where the price of beef had fallen to a disastrous $1.50 per carcass compared with $9 in the boom days.

Foreign investment has never been attempted on the same scale since, yet every now and again a new scare flares up. In 1978 *Business Week* led with the headline 'Foreign Investors Flock to US Farmlands', and the following year a *Time* cover story was headed 'The Foreign Land Grab Scare'. This Reds-under-the-bed sensitivity would appear on the face of things to be scarcely justified. *Business Week* claimed that there was $800 million of foreign capital in US farmland or somewhere near 12 million acres. The total acreage of the USA amounts to 2.3 billion acres, so foreign investment represented rather less than 1 per cent. Just the same, unease appears to have continued to exist, largely arising from an underlying fear that land was being purchased through nominees, thus avoiding the Foreign Investment Disclosure Act passed in 1978.

Who does own this vast tract of land which is America? Basically, in the beginning all the land in the USA was owned by the state, either by simple acquisition or by purchase, starting with the purchase of

Manhattan Island in 1662 from the resident Indians for various trinkets estimated to be worth $24. The historic Louisiana Purchase in 1803 from France, consisting of more than 800,000 square miles between the Rocky Mountains and the Mississippi, for $15 million, would appear to have been quite a bargain. On the other hand in 1867 Russia sold Alaska, a matter of 586,412 square miles, for $7.2 million – but that was before the Klondike Gold Rush!

Once acquired, federal land holdings were distributed in a variety of ways, rather after the fashion of successive English kings of the Middle Ages. Today land holdings are distributed as follows:

	Millions of acres
Private land holdings	34
Grants to veterans	61
Grants to railroads	91
Homesteaders	237
Grants to states	330
Others – mostly cash sales	338
TOTAL	1091

Of the remainder, 762 million acres are still in the public domain, and the total of 2.3 billion acres is made up by 442 million acres which for some reason or other never entered the public domain.

When it comes to discovering who are the leading private land-owners there is the difficulty that, unlike in Britain, there never has been any attempt at a land census. Estimates which have been made from time to time, and never publicly denied, show Nelson Bunker Hunt as by far the single biggest private landowner, with a personal holding of 3.5 million acres. The private land holding of Robert O. Anderson, chairman of the Atlantic Richfield Company, is said to exceed a million acres of Texas. Texas also boasts the biggest single ranch in the country, the King Ranch, which extends to 823,403 acres. There are families such as the Lykes, who own almost half a million acres of Florida and another quarter of a million in the Big Bend country of Texas; there is the Phipps family, which owns extensive land up the eastern seaboard and whose acreage has never been assessed; and famous family dynasties like the Coes and Pingrees of Maine and New Hampshire, whose reported ownership of one million-plus acres is shared amongst some two hundred descendants.

It is, however, when we come to look at the holdings of the big corporations that the question of who really owns America becomes clearer. By far the largest are the oil companies, and a list of the largest of these was published in *Town and Country* magazine in 1983:

	Total acreage
Exxon	40,200,000
Standard Oil of Indiana	29,700,000
Gulf Oil Corporation	15,300,000
Mobil Oil Corporation	12,300,000
Texaco	12,000,000
Shell Oil Company	9,500,000
Phillips Petroleum	9,200,000
Standard Oil of California	7,500,000
Continental Oil (Conoco)	5,300,000
Union Oil	4,900,000

The next group of landowning giants are the paper companies. The top ten of these, again to quote from *Town and Country*, are given as:

	Total acreage
Kimberly-Clark	12,500,000
Burlington Northern	8,600,000
International Paper	8,200,000
Union Pacific Corporation	7,900,000
Weyerhaeuser	6,200,000
Boise-Cascade	6,000,000
Southern Pacific Company	5,200,000
Georgia Pacific	5,100,000
St Regis Paper Company	4,500,000
Crown Zellerbach	2,800,000

In a way the second table of figures is more impressive than the first in that the paper companies, unlike the oil companies, usually own the full surface rights to all their land, whereas the oil and gas companies often own only the mineral rights.

Just the same, a total of 212,900,000 acres owned by twenty top industrial companies is an impressive one indeed in a country which likes to regard itself as primarily agricultural – with some justification as, certainly during the 1970s, food was reckoned to be its biggest export. But in a way the boom in food production became counter-productive. It led to many farming areas planting more and more crops to cash in on the lucrative food export market with the result, as one expert, Charles E. Little, co-author of *The American Cropland Crisis*, puts it, that many American farmers 'beat the hell out of their land.' This has caused the decline and erosion of topsoil at a rate of up to 20 tons per acre.

Added to the demands of industry for more and more land is the recurrent American problem of soil erosion, largely caused by water shortage and droughts. It is estimated that erosion is costing America 3 million acres of cropland a year and that a further 3 million acres are being lost by what they call 'reverse immigration' – people who emigrated to urban centres returning to the country and occupying prime farming land with housing development. The Department of Agriculture state that there only remain 52 million acres of prime agricultural land to be developed, so that if loss of agricultural land continues at the rate of 6 million acres a year, to quote Little again: 'We will be out of our capacity to expand our agriculture within the next 10 to 15 years.'

It is against this background that the former US Secretary of the Interior, James G. Watt, who took office in 1981, became one of the most controversial figures in the Reagan administration. This was largely on account of his declared policy of opening up as many of the federally owned 762 million acres as he could. The opposition to Watt's policy sprang from his intention to lease off vast acreages for oil and coal exploration. These included designated federal Wilderness Areas, which are the rough equivalent of Britain's National Parks, although on a vastly greater scale. Not unnaturally, this sparked off widespread opposition from various environmental bodies with a strong lobby in Congress. Their influence has already halted plans to open up the entire outer continental shelf, amounting to almost a billion acres, to oil and gas interests.

All in all, the American concern with the conservation of their natural environmental heritage is natural and proper. How far the private landowners will be able not only to expand their farmlands but to arrest the advance of the scorched earth frontiers remains to be seen.

12

Where Are We Going?

When compared in size with the 2.3 billion acres which make up the United Staes of America, the British Isles are very small beer indeed. The total land area amounts to some 32,056 million acres in England, 19,070 million in Scotland and 5,099 million in Wales, while Northern Ireland has 3,332 million acres.

All land in Britain is owned by somebody or, to put it more accurately, all land in Britain is subject to rights in one form or another. Even the limited amount of common land is subject to inherent rights, as we have seen. Frequently, the same land offers different rights to different people. Thus an area of land may give one man the right to collect rent for it, another the right to farm it and another the right to shoot over it. To own the freehold of land is to own a bundle of rights which can effectively exclude any other party setting foot upon it. In many cases, however, easements such as rights of way or rights of access can apply. The rigour with which rights are insisted upon varies widely according to the attitude of mind of the owner. Any suburban road contains houses whose front gates are adorned with notices such as 'No Parking' and 'Beware of the Dog', just as, amongst larger property owners, there are some who insist on their privacy with greater vehemence by profuse use of 'Trespassers Will Be Prosecuted' notices.

There are four main demands made on the land, regardless of in whose ownership it happens to be: the need to produce food; the need to produce timber; urban development requirements; and recreation. The competition for land is naturally much more intense in England and Wales than it is in Scotland, where the full effects of the postwar population explosion have not yet been felt and where there are still large areas available for development in response to these four needs. However, the trends in the south will eventually expand to the more remote areas as the pressures increase, so an examination of the current position in England and Wales may be taken as setting the pattern for the future, bearing in mind that the trend is for agricultural land to be steadily lost for alternative uses such as industrial or urban development. The loss is estimated as being in the region of 60,000 acres a year.

The proportion of land devoted to forestry and woodland can be fairly accurately estimated at around 9 per cent. In the last ten years the percentages owned by the Forestry Commission and private land-owners have altered considerably so that where they started out in the early 'seventies as almost even, with a slightly bigger holding in the private sector, today the Commission controls almost two-thirds of all afforested land. Every now and again a new row breaks out between various conservationist bodies and the Commission over the acquisition of National Park land for afforestation. This conflict of interests is hard to resolve, particularly when economists point to the increasing need for timber, notably hardwoods, in the years to come and to the importance of reducing Britain's dependence on foreign imports, which are currently running at around 90 per cent. To set against this, in practice the demand for softwoods continues to be much greater than the demand for hardwoods, despite much propaganda to the contrary. It is also worth noting that in the last three years the Forestry Commission has been selling off substantial portions of its more isolated plantations in the Midlands and the south of England.

It is generally estimated that 12 per cent of Britain's land has already been used for urban development and that the need is constantly increasing. This figure, together with afforested land, leaves a total of 80 per cent devoted to agriculture, which represents roughly the same acreage as the land holdings of the Exxon Corporation in the USA! This figure can be broken down with some accuracy into different categories, which will give some indication of the direction in which Britain is going.

At the end of the First World War, as the country prepared to enter another period of agricultural depression, only about 10 per cent of all agricultural land was owner-occupied. Today the figure is nearer 70 per cent. Of the remaining 30 per cent at least a third is owned by the increasing number of 'institutional' investors; the balance consists of farms rented out by landowners. Today there is very little land changing hands – about 3 per cent in a normal year, although since 1985 it has not even reached this figure. The greater part of this land is traded inside the farming community itself; with institutional buying limited to let land only, of which an ever smaller proportion, perhaps as little as 25 per cent, meets their investment criteria.

As recently as 1957 Dr D. R. Denman of Cambridge University wrote in his book *Estate Capital* that the traditional reasons for owning land, such as inheritance, residential and social responsibility, were still the most valid ones, and that purely monetary considerations took second place. This view is now hopelessly out of date. Exactly how monetary the considerations are is demonstrated by the intensity of interest amongst City and institutional investors.

The Church, which rates amongst the largest in the landowners' league, caused an outcry in the 1970s, as has already been observed in Chapter 8, by selling off a great deal of their lower-rented rural property in order to invest in high income-producing bricks and mortar. The outcry was turned into something like outrage amongst their tenants in London's Maida Vale by a proposal to raise their rentals by some 85 per cent. It was all part of a rationalization plan to bring the hitherto rather unworldly attitude of the Church into the twentieth century. By the same token, during the 1970s the average rent per acre on farmland rose by 208 per cent, as opposed to a rise of a mere 71 per cent in stocks and shares over the same period. Sir Ronald Harris, then First Commissioner for the Church Estates, said in 1983: 'Agricultural land has undoubtedly proved one of the best forms of investment from the point of view of preserving and enhancing capital value and securing a reliable and growing income.' When one considers that in the last century monetary considerations had no place at all, the extent of the revolution which has taken place can be readily appreciated.

And to the future? There would seem to be little ground for the unease felt by some landowners over the repeated mutterings on the Labour benches on the subject of the nationalization of land. Indeed when the Labour Government was in power most of the land legislation it introduced was designed to protect the landowners rather than the opposite, in return for their giving greater access to the Government's largely urban-based supporters.

With the growing trend for land to become owner-occupied has also come a great leap forward in efficiency and productivity. This has, of course, been partly due to advanced technology, which in turn results in a sharp drop in labour costs and the tendency for more and more farms to become multiples; but this then means that the farmer should be in a position where he can invest in capital goods. This again, has led in economic terms to a substantial increase in the acreage of an economically viable farm, which is now around 350 acres, and equally to a very substantial drop in the number of people employed in agriculture.

Although the great estates of the eighteenth and nineteenth centuries are now a relic of the past, the crofter and smallholder have also largely disappeared. Holdings of under 200 acres are not in a position to compete with farms of larger acreages and with the multiples, because they cannot support the capital investment required.

The attitude of successive Governments towards urban landowners, not excluding the administrators of large acreages of nationalized land like the British Rail Property Board or the Port of London Authority, has not been seen to be either benign or consistent. Whilst City institutions range ever further afield in search of agricultural purchase, there seems to be a reluctance to allow public authorities owning land to develop it to the best interests of their shareholders as represented by the general public. At the same time, the introduction of legislation to enable long-standing owners of leaseholds on the large private estates, like Cadogan and Westminster, to purchase their freeholds might have some sort of democratic justification, but this policy cannot but lead in the long run to a lowering of general standards in the better administered areas.

The voice of the property speculator is not now heard in the land – perhaps sadly, despite his many critics. Today virtually all new property development is being undertaken with the backing and equity involvement of the institutions.

Let us now look at the variations in agricultural land values since the immediate postwar period. To assess *exact* variations is for a variety of reasons not practical. The pioneer work in this field, started in 1945 by D. K. Britton and J. T. Ward and carried on by authorities like G. H. Peters, was conducted principally using source material from *The Estates Gazette*. Known as the Oxford Institute Series, these studies have been, with some justice, criticized for being too heavily weighted with sales in the Home Counties and ignoring sales below a certain acreage.

A further survey conducted by the Inland Revenue and derived from stamp duty records has also come under criticism, mainly on the grounds that the time which inevitably elapsed from the date of contract to the payment of duty often put sales not only in a later month from the one in which they had actually taken place, but in a later year. This was a serious deficiency when, in the volatile state of the market, trends should have been discernible on a much more day-to-day basis.

In the early 1970s the Country Landowners' Association started their own survey, largely based on sampling; in order to arrive at more accurate and immediate figures the CLA joined in 1980 with the Agricultural Mortgage Corporation and the Agricultural Development and Advisory Service, although sales of as little as twelve acres are included in the statistics.

Even allowing for all these factors which militate against exactness, the general trends are unmistakable. *The Oxford Institute* figures, which go back to 1949, are given overleaf. They apply only to land with vacant possession.

In 1976 there started the dramatic rise in land prices which peaked, according to the Oxford Institute Series, in 1983. The ADAS/AMC/CLA version shows almost exactly the same peak, £2,044 an acre against £2,032, being reached in February 1984, their figures being given on a monthly rather than an annual basis. Both surveys, however, agree that land prices are now experiencing another

slide similar to that which occurred in the mid-1970s, but for quite
different reasons.

	£/acre		£/acre
1949	76	1967	258
1950	80	68	280
51	88	69	299
52	76	1970	245*
53	73	71	262
54	75	72	596
55	80	73	757
56	78	74	636†
57	73	75	539
58	85	76	734
59	101	77	991
1960	123	78	1,327
61	124	79	1,769
62	134	1980	1,726
63	168	81	1,729
64	214	82	1,844
65	235	83	2,082
66	242	84	1,978

* The seeming temporary reversal of the general trend was due simply to the
introduction of a new method of assessment.
† The prices in the three years following 1973 were due to the effects of the new oil
industry and general political uncertainty.

Put at its most simple, the reason for the sharp rise to an
unprecedented land value of over £2,000 an acre, and for the current
slide, may be attributed to our entry into the Common Market in 1974.
We have seen that the first dramatic rise in land prices in the 'fifties to
the mid-'seventies was due to the effects of modern technology enabling
drastic reductions in labour costs, whilst at the same time greatly
increasing productivity.

Of all British industry, agriculture is by far the most efficient. It is
also more efficient than the same industry in any other member
country in the EEC – which in effect means in any other country in the
world. It was this efficiency, translated into terms of prosperity, which
made it possible for farmers to pay higher rentals and which, in turn,
inspired the rush of investment money from institutions and the City.

Just the same, in the mid-1970s Britain was still importing 40 per
cent of its requirements of agricultural produce such as corn, milk, beef,
sugar and mutton. Indeed, as an example, the whole of New Zealand's

economy was, and still is, geared to the export to the UK of its mutton and butter.

By the end of the 1970s Britain had become a net exporter of agricultural produce. The boom experienced in farming on joining the EEC was based largely on the fact that we could take advantage of our greater agricultural efficiency, and consequent lower cost of production of food, with a substantial leeway to make up on the price of corn, milk and sugar. In fact, our home subsidies, or direct grant payments, were broadly in line with those applying in the EEC. It should also be remarked that 70 per cent of the whole of the EEC budget was devoted to agriculture in the late 1970s and early 1980s, although this figure has dropped substantially with the increase in world grain prices, reducing the cost of subsidizing the EEC surplus.

It was a policy which, when applied to the UK, resulted in projecting any farmer with a freeholding of over 1,000 acres into millionaire and double millionaire status, at least on paper, whilst large landowners and the big multiple farmers could vie with the richest of industrialists and City magnates. Land ownership became, for the first time in its history, the richest source of wealth in its own right, independent of mineral wealth, urban property or even the necessity of contracting marriages!

It was predictable that this should evoke, to put it mildly, political unease, which broke into major controversy when it became increasingly clear, by 1984, that production was moving into substantial surplus year by year. This increased the pressure to sell grain 'into intervention' under the EEC guaranteed price system, leading to a situation where very substantial surpluses of almost 5 million tons of grain were being carried forward into 1985. This represented a value in money terms of around £500 million of Government money, to which should be added the very considerable cost of storage.

By the terms of the intervention clause the Government was bound to buy at a guaranteed price farmers' surplus production for which no other legitimate market could be found. With the national production wound up to such a high level the momentum could not be reversed overnight; every storage facility was rapidly filled to overflowing. Nor was there any outlet. It was an inherent part of the agreed EEC policy that each country should be required to absorb its own surplus, despite the fact that the USSR provided a ready market of which our less scrupulous partners in the EEC availed themselves *de la main gauche*. Even to ship surpluses to the starving areas of the world was prohibited. In the event the situation, which had reached crisis proportions by the spring of 1985, was saved by the failure of the harvest. At the same time, however, a similar situation had been created by the over-production of milk. The much-mocked problem which had already arisen amongst our European partners, who had produced wine lakes and butter mountains, had suddenly landed on our own doorstep.

Looked at practically, the main problem was simply that nobody could find an answer to what to do with the huge surpluses created by our own agricultural efficiency. The only possible solution was to curb production of those products in surplus, particularly wheat, barley and milk. It was this situation which caused the Ministry of Agriculture in 1985 to bow as much to expediency as to political pressure by introducing the quota system for milk production which has had the effect of reducing production by 20 per cent, but has also raised all manner of economic problems for dairy farmers, particularly those with smaller acreages whose operations ceased to be economically viable under their revised quotas. At the same time a process was begun of persuading the big grain-producing farmers, who had profited so mightily under the subsidy system, to go back into beef production.

The then Minister of Agriculture, Mr Jopling, received a tepid round of applause for persuading his Common Market colleagues that part of the obligatory 70 per cent injection of money into agriculture could be syphoned off from subsidizing food production and used instead for the 'amelioration' of the countryside. This means in effect that, instead of paying landowners or farmers (the description nowadays is becoming more and more synonymous) heavy subsidies to produce unwanted food, part of the money could be used to pay them to replant hedges and restore other such eye-pleasing features instead of bulldozing everything in sight in favour of more and more earth space for food production.

About three-quarters of all home-produced food is produced by a quarter of our farms. Far from bearing out the contention of those persistent snipers at landed privilege who maintain that all the land and all the power is in the hands of a tiny section of the community – the exact percentages depending on the prejudices of the commentator – this figure shows precisely the opposite. It demonstrates just how far the picture of twentieth-century landownership has moved from the time of Lord Derby's survey, a hundred years earlier, which showed, however inaccurately, that about three-quarters of all the land was vested in some seven thousand individuals.

In this connection it might be of some interest to list the great estates of the 1870s, together with their acreages and rentals. The table opposite shows that approximately 7,500,000 acres was owned by a mere thirty-five individuals. It will not have escaped the reader, however, that not only have many of the names of the larger estate owners disappeared completely from the present-day scene, but

	Acres	£ rental
Duke of Argyll	175,114	50,812
Duke of Atholl	194,640	40,758
Evan Baillie of Dochfour	165,648	17,581
Earl of Breadalbane	438,358	58,292
Duke of Buccleuch	458,739	216,026
Marquis of Bute	116,668	231,421
Cameron of Lochiel	126,008	10,721
Earl of Cawdor	101,657	44,662
The Chisholm	113,256	8,779
Duke of Cleveland	104,194	97,398
Earl of Dalhousie	138,021	58,603
Duke of Devonshire	198,665	180,990
James Farquharson of Invercauld	107,801	11,075
Earl of Fife	259,003	79,831
Earl Fitzwilliam	115,743	138,801
John Gordon of Cluny	112,354	31,188
Sir G. Macpherson-Grant Bt	125,443	11,546
Duke of Hamilton and Brandon	157,386	73,636
Earl of Home	106,550	56,632
Marquis of Lansdowne	142,916	63,025
Lord Leconfield	109,935	88,112
Lord Macdonald of Skye	129,919	11,613
Sir Kenneth Mackenzie of Gairloch	164,680	7,842
The MacLeod of Dunvegan	141,679	8,464
Alexander Matheson (Ross-shire)	220,663	22,386
Sir James Matheson (Isle of Lewis)	424,560	19,488
Duke of Montrose	103,760	23,069
Duke of Northumberland	186,397	176,048
Duke of Portland	162,235	124,925
Duke of Richmond and Gordon	286,411	79,683
Sir Charles Ross of Balnagowan	166,866	15,133
Earl of Seafield	305,930	72,079
Earl of Stair	116,370	61,905
Duke of Sutherland	1,358,546	141,679
Baroness Willoughby de Eresby	136,680	79,149

reference to rentals readily shows that most of these vast estates consisted of little more than rock, heather and sheep land. A much more significant statistic today is that three-quarters of all productive agricultural land is in the hands of the smaller owner-occupiers or tenants.

The effect of the present curbs in food production on the very big producers is not likely to be economically disastrous, but the same cannot be said about the smaller units. A disproportionate number of them are dairy farms, and here the 10 per cent cut in production is having a very serious effect. This happens particularly in cases where the quota has been assessed on a previous year's production which was artificially low, due to the many ills and misfortunes to which the dairy farmer in particular seems to be heir. In extreme cases it might even mean selling up, probably to a 'big brother' neighbour who could with advantage take over the quota to add to his own and would be glad of some extra grazing. Thus the tendency could be for the bigger unit to get bigger and for some of the smaller land holdings to disappear altogether.

The French farmer, faced with a limitation of quota, will by his very character seek a means of mitigating it or avoiding it. He is almost certain to be supported in this by his Government, who will undoubtedly be exploring export guarantees, import standards and a host of other technical details to ensure that the French farmer's produce can continue to sell at competitive prices and his surpluses be disposed of, while still operating generally within the EEC umbrella. Thus he goes on happily producing his mountains of cereals and lakes of milk, relatively unconcerned at the fuss going on around him.

The effect of these substantial food surpluses, the attendant introduction of quotas and reduction of guaranteed prices, has inevitably had a substantial effect on farm profitability. As land prices are themselves directly related to the profits to be derived from farming, it is not difficult to see the reason behind the recent slide in land prices. In fact, when inflation is taken into account, land values have declined relatively rapidly from a peak in 1979, in many instances by as much as 40 per cent of their real worth over the last five years. This is not always directly reflected in the statistical analyses of farmland prices currently available; such statistics can take no account of the fact that, in a declining market, only the best land will sell readily, which tends to paint an inflated picture of prices overall.

During 1987 this trend has continued with marginal fluctuations. In practice, however, the decline in values is likely to be most marked on the least productive and marginal land, the stock-rearing land and hill farms, the small dairy units in the south-west, and those areas where soil quality, rainfall, drainage and height above sea level inhibit the economic production of arable crops or milk. This decline in land values is unlikely to affect the very best land, which amounts to only some 25 per cent of all land farmed in this country. Looking to the future, this trend is likely to continue, with an increasing proportion of the marginal land going out of food production altogether, and with increasing pressures for alternative uses such as recreation, forestry and sport. These policies will inevitably have a major and lasting effect on rural communities in hill farm and stock-farming areas, where no consistent alternative sources of livelihood are available, either now or in the foreseeable future.

This trend in values has also applied to tenanted land, which peaked in 1980 and has been steadily dropping in value in real terms ever since. While the uncertainties of the EEC surpluses remain, farming profits continue to be under pressure; and while rental growth is, in consequence, likely to be limited, the prospect of a major return to the market by the financial institutions is slight. Nevertheless, as the restriction in guaranteed food subsidies is reduced within the EEC, so a great percentage of marginal land will be taken out of production, and with an increasing concentration on low-cost farming in the more commercial units the problem of surpluses may yet disappear.

Despite rumblings from the left wing threatening such drastic measures as land nationalization, successive Governments have shown an increasing concern in preserving heritable assets. A good example is the alleniation of the once onerous capital transfer tax which led to the break-up of many fine estates that had been so assiduously preserved from generation to generation.

It is not generally realized that legislation like the Finance Act of 1975 and more recently the Wildlife and Countryside Act of 1981 does not operate solely for the protection of the owners of the great stately homes. The striking concessions of the 1975 Finance Act in alleviating liability for capital transfer tax was designed to benefit landowners on a far wider basis than is generally understood. Basically the Act made graded concessions according to whether the transfer was made in the lifetime of the incumbent or only at death, but there were many other means by which exemption or partial exemption could be achieved. Owners of properties of quite modest proportions – be they of scenic beauty, of scientific or historical interest such as ancient monuments, or even old battle sites – can qualify at the discretion of the Treasury if public access is given, just as the stateliest of stately homes can claim exemption by opening its doors to the public. In practice even the most limited 'by appointment only' access can qualify for exemption. It is long-sighted and sensible to encourage landowners to permit their land to be enjoyed by the general public and meet the increasing demand for leisure facilities.

Looking at the first edition of *The Landowners*, written in 1964, I see that the final paragraph reads:

> There is no doubt that the landowner–tenant relationship, which has been preserved nowhere as it has been in Britain, is a formula from which many benefits have flowed in the past and from which they can continue to flow. That there have been bad landowners cannot be denied and no doubt there will be bad landowners in the future. On the whole, however, it is the good forward-looking landowners who have prevailed and whose example has been followed, however reluctantly, by the backsliders. They have been the source of a constant flow of fresh capital, which has buffered their tenants in

misfortune and enabled them to become more productive over the years, so that today the record of the agriculturalist in this country is second to none in the world. In contrast to other sections of industry in this country, farmers set an example by continually increasing production while using less land and employing fewer people. Less tangibly, landowners continue to support a dignified way of life which has set a valuable standard in the past and can continue to do so in the future.

Looking at the picture almost a quarter of a century later, I can see no real reason to change those views.

Index of places

Index of personal names